MARY FORD

The Complete Book of Soft Toys

With step-by-step instructions and full-size templates

Contents

☆ Star Ratings ☆

All soft toys are graded for ease of making: one star being suitable for
beginners, through to four or five stars for the experienced soft toy maker.

Introduction

Soft toy making is a pleasurable and rewarding activity which can easily become a profitable hobby. This book, which is for both the beginner and the experienced toy maker is a structured, step-by-step course on toy-making covering glove puppets, soft toys and teddy bears. Toys are graded from one to five stars to indicate the degree of expertise involved, one being the easiest and most suitable for the beginner. Each toy is accompanied by a full size cutting template and instructions together with a colour photograph of the finished toy. Every step is clearly illustrated by a photograph and there are easy to follow instructions on the simple techniques and materials required for a professional result. Inexperienced toy-makers will find that careful study of the preliminary stages and working instructions will avoid many of the faults and difficulties caused by incorrect materials or too hasty working.

The 30 toys in this book have been specially designed by Anne Sexton, the well-known soft toy maker. They are made from the best quality materials to high safety standards. The eyes and noses used are all of the washered type and the toys, if made to the instructions, are easily kept clean.

The finished toy will bring hours of fun to a child - as something to fire the imagination in play and as a friend to cuddle. And a great sense of pride to *you* as the maker.

AUTHORS

MARY FORD's highly successful cake artistry books have sold over 900,000 copies worldwide. Her unique step-by-step approach with the emphasis on self-explanatory colour illustrations has been successfully adapted to soft toys for this book. Mary has had a life-long interest in traditional crafts and after meeting Anne Sexton at a craft fair they decided to work together on bringing the step-by-step format to craft making.

MICHAEL FORD once again works with his wife on this book as photographer and editor.

ANNE SEXTON is a professional toy-maker with a reputation for quality and inventive designs. She made soft toys for her own children when they were young and then turned her hobby into a successful career. She now exhibits extensively at craft fairs throughout the south of England and her toys are exported all over the world.

© Mary Ford Publications Ltd.

First published as "Soft Toys" (1990), "Glove Puppets" (1991)
and "Teddy Bears" (1991)

This Edition Published 1997

ISBN: 0946429 60 X

Materials and Tools

Materials:

MATERIALS should always be selected for quality, durability and appeal. The character of the finished toy will be greatly enhanced by the use of an appropriate colour and texture. When purchasing materials, it is also important to ensure that they comply with the statutory regulations for the safety of children's toys.

Note: For photographic purposes, a contrasting thread has been used to show the stitching line throughout this book. However, a matching or toning thread should be used when sewing the toys.

FUR FABRIC

A fur fabric with a supple knitted backing is ideal for soft toys as it stretches slightly and does not fray. A good quality fur has dense pile through which the backing is not visible - when a hand is run against the pile, the backing material should not show through. The patterns in this book all have instructions as to the type of fur fabric required.
- Polished fur has a short, shiny pile
- Plush fur has a thicker, shorter pile
- Long haired fur has a longer, polished pile
- Mohair has a short, dense pile and is made from the hair of a Tibetan goat. It is used for the traditional teddy and whilst it does not stretch and is much more expensive than the other furs, it produces an exceptionally high-quality finish for the experienced needlewoman.
- Special furs include 'spotty' and 'tiger'

FELT

Felt can be purchased in a wide range of colours in small squares or from the roll. Polyester felt is not a strong fabric, but it is washable and can be used for lining ears or making feet and beaks.

LINING

Suitable soft material should be used for linings and clothes.

FILLING

Hi loft polyester filling is recommended as it is washable, springy and non-allergic. Foam chips should not be used as tiny pieces of foam can easily be inhaled by small children and the finished toy will have a lumpy appearance.

THREAD

A strong toning synthetic thread should be used for sewing seams as this will not break when the toy is turned and filled. Button, or extra-strong thread should be used for sewing the head in place and, after stuffing, for closing the seam. Stranded embroidery thread should be used for facial features.

Tools:

THE right tool for the job is essential. Gather together all materials and tools prior to cutting and sewing as this makes the work much quicker and easier. Most of the tools required are contained in a dressmaker's kit and all the toys in this book can be made using an ordinary domestic sewing machine.

SCISSORS

A good, sharp pair of scissors is required for cutting fabric. An old pair of scissors should be used for pattern and template cutting. A small, pointed pair of embroidery scissors is also useful.

PAPER AND CARD

Tracing paper should be used for tracing templates, which are then transferred to durable card, (use old cereal packets or Christmas cards). A thin coat of latex fabric adhesive can be used to glue tracing paper to card.

PENS AND PENCILS

A felt tip pen can be used for tracing or drawing on card but can smudge on fabric. A 2B lead pencil is suitable for marking light coloured fabrics and dressmaker's chalk for darker fabrics.

PINS AND NEEDLES

Pins and needles should be counted before and after use to ensure they are not left in the toy where they could injure a child. Extra-long pins with coloured beaded heads should be used. Medium needles are required for hand-sewing and a darning needle for sewing on heads and embroidery. No. 16 or 18 machine needles are the most durable.

STUFFING TOOLS

Most shapes can be stuffed by hand using the fingers, but a screwdriver, unsharpened pencil or the blunt end of a knitting needle can be used for small work.

BRUSHES

A teazle brush is required to bring up the pile of fur fabric after handling or sewing and a clothes brush for brushing the finished toy.

Pattern Making

TEMPLATES

The templates in this book are all full size and ready for the preparation of a pattern on card, as shown pictorially in steps 1-9 below. 'Spot the Dalmatian' is used here as an example but the principle is the same for all pattern making. Always ensure that all markings, instructions, etc., are transferred from each template in the book to the pattern.

NOTE: Due to restrictions on space, some templates are shown drawn inside another one. Each one should be traced onto a separate sheet. Do not cut out smaller template from inside a larger one.

KEY TO PATTERN MARKINGS	
Cutting Line	————
Joining Line	⌣⌢⌣
Stitching Line	— — —
Fold Line	– – – –
Direction of pile or straight of fabric	⇨
Position of eye	●
Position of ears or tail	=
Easing or snipping points	◀

A clearly labelled paper bag or envelope should be used to store the completed pattern.

PATTERN LAYOUT

Having made the pattern, select an appropriate piece of material and, if using fur fabric, check the direction of the pile by running the flat of the hand across the pile. In one direction the pile will be raised up from the surface of the fabric, in the other it will lie smooth. Turn the fabric over, pile side to the table, and mark with an arrow the direction in which the fabric lies smoothly. (On smooth fabric mark the straight of the fabric.) The fabric should be placed on the table so that the pile is lying smoothly towards you. The puppet will then appear to 'stand up' as the patterns are laid out. Do not use the selvedge edge. Match the arrows on the pattern to the arrow indicating pile direction on the fabric so that patterns all lie in the same direction. Position the larger pieces first and then the smaller pieces can be fitted in, remembering to check the direction of the pile. Ensure that all patterns are correctly positioned and that no piece has been omitted.

   Draw around all the patterns, marking light coloured fabric with soft lead pencil and dark fabric with chalk (this is the cutting line). Carefully cut around each pattern with sharp scissors. When using fur fabric, slide the point of the blade under the pile and cut through the backing and gently separate the pieces to avoid damaging the pile. Fur fabric should always be cut through a single thickness only, but felt or lining can be cut as a double thickness where appropriate. Small openings or holes should be made with embroidery scissors.

—— MAKING A PATTERN ——

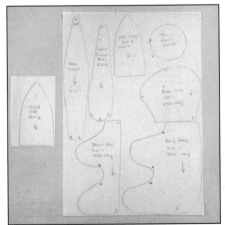

1 Trace the template for the required design from the book onto tracing paper with a pencil, taking care to transfer all markings.

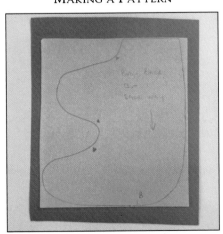

2 Cut a rough square around each shape and then glue the tracing to card.

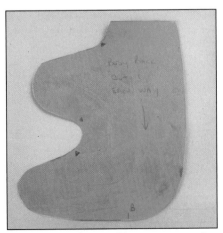

3 Following the pencil line, cut out card shape. Repeat for each pattern piece. Check all markings have been transferred.

FOLD LINE TRACING

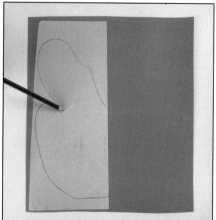

4 *Lay out traced template face down on card (markings towards card) with 'fold line' to centre. Draw around shape, omitting 'fold line.'*

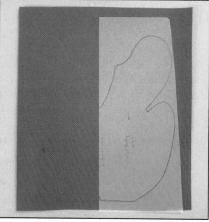

5 *Carefully turn the pattern over, keeping fold line to centre. Glue into position.*

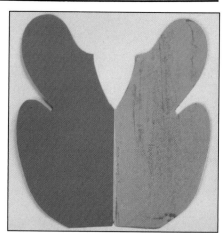

6 *Cut the pattern out as one piece (see KERRY the KOALA on p.33).*

JOINING TEMPLATE PIECES

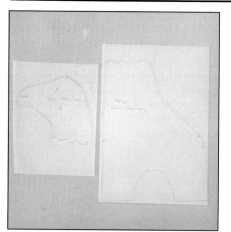

7 *Trace around separate templates on to tracing paper as shown. Cut out and trim along wavy lines (see Jack the Rabbit p.100).*

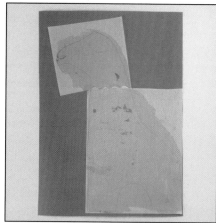

8 *Matching wavy lines as shown, place both pieces of tracing paper on to a single piece of card. Glue on to card.*

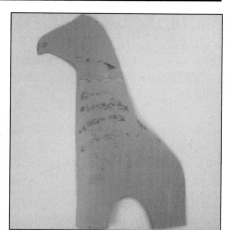

9 *Cut the pattern out as one piece.*

CUT 1 EACH WAY

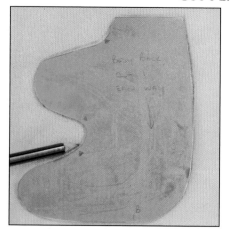

10 *Place the pattern on a single thickness of fabric. Carefully draw around the pattern.*

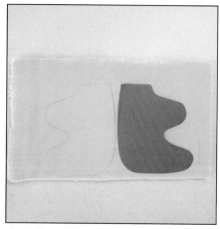

11 *Turn pattern over as shown and draw around pattern shape again. Cut out the two shapes round the cutting line.*

CUT 2

12 *On a single thickness of fabric, lay out pattern and draw around it. Lift pattern, keeping the same side facing, and lay on fabric. Draw around again. Cut out.*

Sewing Techniques

SEAM ALLOWANCE
A seam allowance of 6mm (¼") is included on the pattern pieces.

STITCHING LINE
The stitching line is 6mm (¼") in from the edge of the fabric unless otherwise indicated.

SEAMS
Seams may be sewn by hand or by machine. All the seams shown in this book have been sewn on an ordinary domestic sewing machine and finished by hand oversewing or a zigzag machine stitch. Full sewing instructions are given in the step-by-step guide for each toy.

Throughout the book in the step-by-step instructions seams have been pinned, using extra-long glass-headed pins, and sewn straight from pinning. Beginners could tack the seams before sewing, removing the tacking threads after stitching. For photographic purposes seams have not been finished off but, to ensure that seams do not open, machine stitching should be reversed for approximately 6mm (¼") at each end.

Begin sewing a seam by pinning together the two pieces to be joined, right sides facing together. As each section of seam is sewn, remove pins as appropriate. Fur seams should be brushed out with a teazle brush.

Note: For photographic purposes, a contrasting thread has been used to show the stitching line throughout this book. However, a matching or toning thread should be used when sewing the toys.

EASE POINT
Curved or angled seams may need to be snipped to the stitching line with scissors in order to ease the fabric. Care should be used not to snip the stitching line.

STITCHES
○ Backstitch should be used when sewing seams by hand as this produces a strong seam which will not break.
○ Oversewing or zigzag stitch should be used to prevent fabric fraying.
○ Ladder stitch (See step 5 on page 8) should be used for joining heads to bodies.

THREADS
A matching strong synthetic thread should be used for sewing seams as this will not break when the toy is turned and filled. The end should be knotted firmly when sewing by hand. Thread can be used double for extra strength. Button thread, or other extra-strong thread, should be used for sewing the head, nose, ears or tail in place. Stranded embroidery thread is used for embroidering facial features.

FACIAL FEATURES
Careful placement of the facial features will enhance the puppet's appearance and create the appropriate expression and character.
○ EYES: Most of the toys in this book have been fitted with safety eyes (See steps 6-9 on page 8). Safety eyes are available in different styles and sizes and sold complete with plastic or metal washers. When using a knitted fabric, stitch around the hole before the eye is fitted to ensure safety. (See step 7 on page 8).
○ NOSES: Several different styles and sizes of noses are available. Noses can also be made from felt or fabric or embroidered directly on to the fabric (see steps 1-4 on page 8).
○ SQUEAKERS AND RATTLES: Steps 11-17 on page 31 (*Quackers the Duck*) illustrate the fitting of a squeaker. Other instructions are given in the step-by-step guide to each toy where appropriate.

TURNING AND STUFFING
All seams should be carefully inspected, and the eyes inserted if necessary, before turning right side out. The head should be gently eased through the opening. When turning a full body, the limbs should be turned using the fingers, or a blunt stuffing tool, and then the limbs should be eased through the body opening.

If required, insert the nose before stuffing the toy. Stuff carefully in accordance with the directions given in the step-by-step instructions. Always stuff slightly harder than required as the stuffing will soften when handled.

MONKEY MOUTH

1 Bring the needle out at bottom of nose and embroider a line down. Insert needle, come out to the left, then back to bottom. Repeat for the right side.

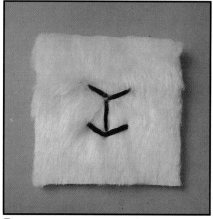

BUNNY NOSE AND MOUTH

2 Work three stitches as for Monkey Mouth, then take needle out at top of straight stitch. Work angled stitches to left and right to match bottom.

TEDDY MOUTH

3 Bring needle out at top of nose, embroider a straight line down. Insert needle and come out one-third of the way to the left as shown. Take needle back to bottom of the long the stitch and repeat for right side.

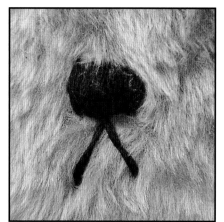

TEDDY NOSE AND MOUTH

4 Make a series of long parallel stitches close together to form the nose, slightly decreasing size at ends. Repeat. Make two long, angled stitches as shown for the mouth.

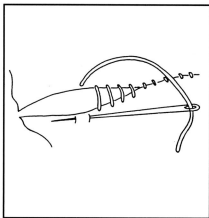

LADDER STITCH

5 Using strong thread, make small stitch 6mm (¼") on side of opening. Make a small stitch on other side. Repeat to end. Pull up tightly and secure.

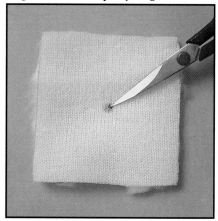

FITTING SAFETY EYES AND NOSES

6 Make a very small hole at eye position marked using small pointed scissors.

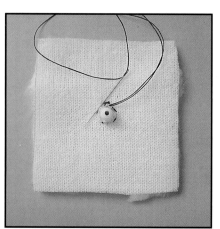

7 Push shank of eye through from right side of material. Turn to right side and check position on the face. On stretchy material, stitch around opening.

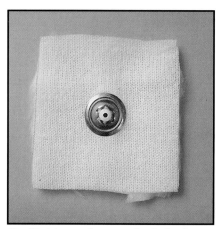

8 Position washer over shank. Lock washer against back of eye pressing down hard, keeping the washer level, to engage the teeth against shank.

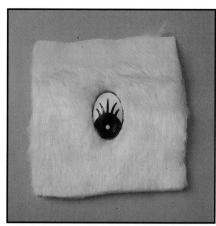

9 With right side facing, gently ease out any fur which has become trapped around the eye.

JOINTS

JOINTED Teddy Bears with moveable arms and legs, and heads that swivel from side to side, greatly add to the appeal and play potential of the toy for children. The old style of joints were very complicated as they required a cotter pin and discs. However, the new style joint available today is simple to fix and is readily available in handicraft shops.

A joint with a diameter appropriate to the size of the Teddy Bear should be selected. When attaching a limb, the limb should be sewn and stuffed half way first, leaving the top of the seam open. Insert peg from inside the limb through the joint hole. The stuffing should then be completed and the seam closed with ladder stitch. Attach the limb to the body as shown in steps 1-6 below.

When attaching the head, run a gathering stitch around the neck opening. Insert joint into the neck opening, leaving the peg outside, and pull up the gathering thread tightly. Fix the head to the body by pushing the peg through the small opening in the top of the body, securing with plastic and metal safety washers (See pages 189 and 190, steps 35-37).

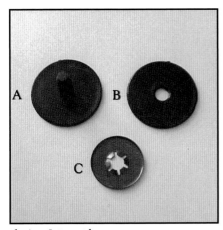

1 A – *Joint with peg.*
B – *Plastic washer.*
C – *Metal safety washer.*
All three sections are required for each limb or head to be attached.

2 Sew a running stitch around the hole position on the body and on the limb. Carefully snip the hole with sharp, pointed scissors.

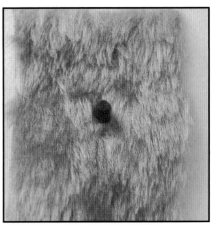

3 Insert the joint A into the limb, working from the wrong side of the fabric, so that the peg protrudes through to the right side as shown.

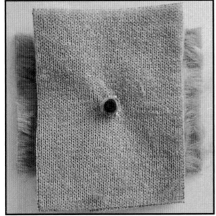

4 Insert the peg, working from the right side of the fabric, into the hole in the body as shown.

5 Place the plastic washer B over the peg and push down firmly until locked.

6 Place the metal safety washer C onto the peg and push down as far as possible. Ensure that it is level.

FINGER MOUSE ☆

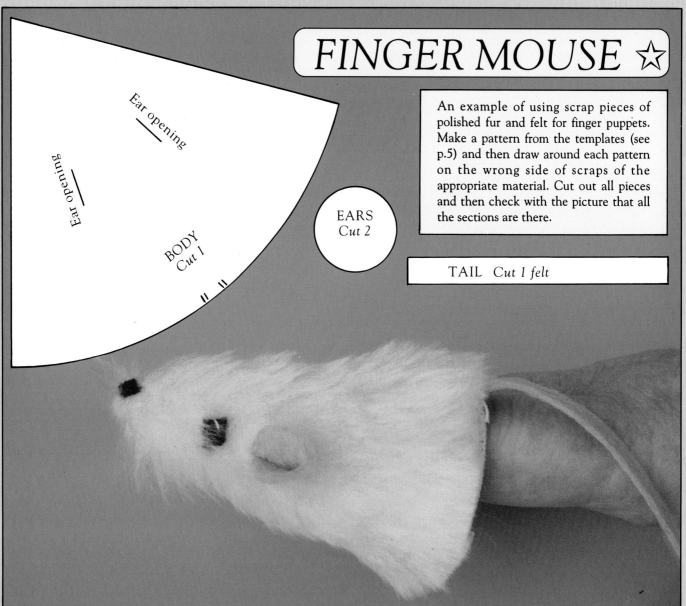

Ear opening

Ear opening

BODY
Cut 1

EARS
Cut 2

An example of using scrap pieces of polished fur and felt for finger puppets. Make a pattern from the templates (see p.5) and then draw around each pattern on the wrong side of scraps of the appropriate material. Cut out all pieces and then check with the picture that all the sections are there.

TAIL Cut 1 felt

1 Fold ears in half and pin. Cut ear openings and insert folded ear into each side. Pin and stitch in position.

2 Fold in half, right sides facing, and pin along straight edge. Stitch together.

3 Turn right side out and brush seam. Stitch on tail and then small circles of felt for the eyes and nose.

SID the SNAKE ☆

MATERIALS

○ Green Polished Fur 300mm (12″) × 350mm (14″).

○ Green Felt 230mm (9″) × 125mm (5″).

○ Lining 125mm (5″) × 125mm (5″).

○ 1 Rattle.

○ 2 Small Black Eyes.

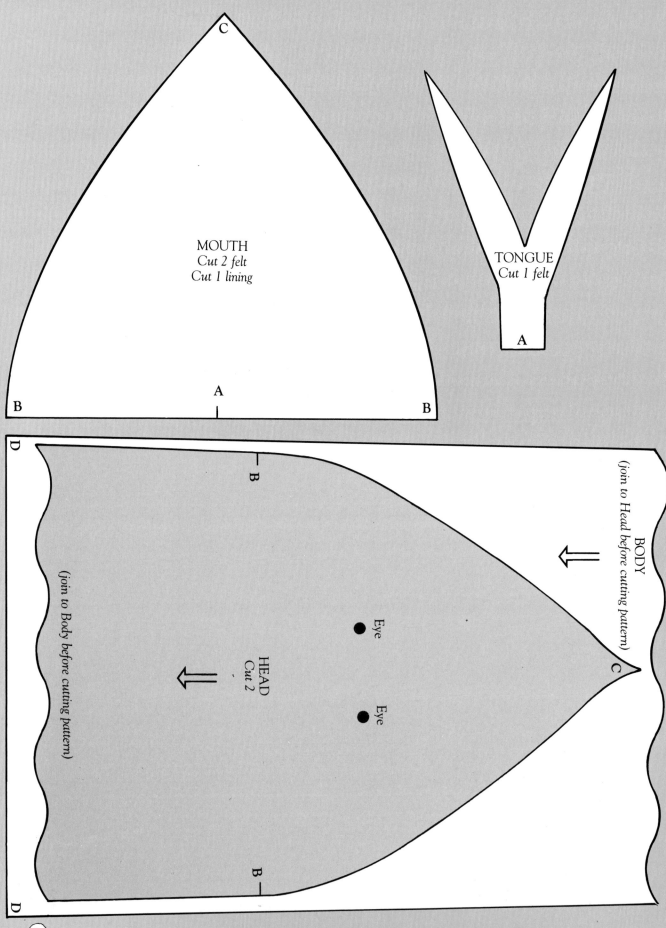

MOUTH
Cut 2 felt
Cut 1 lining

TONGUE
Cut 1 felt

A

C

B   A   B

D   B

BODY
(join to Head before cutting pattern)

● Eye

● Eye

HEAD
Cut 2

C

(join to Body before cutting pattern)

B

D

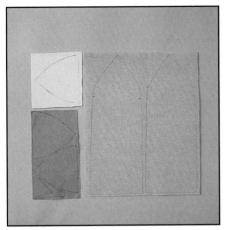

1 Make a pattern of each template shape required (see p.5). Then draw around each pattern on the wrong side of the appropriate material, as shown.

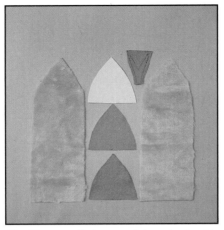

2 Cut out all pieces and then check with the picture that all the sections are there.

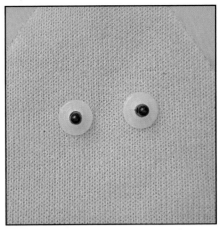

3 Insert eyes (see p.8) in marked position on head.

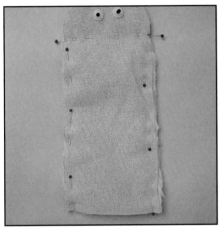

4 Place the two bodies together, right sides facing. Pin from **D** to **B** and then **B** to **D**.

5 Stitch from **B** to **D** on each side of the body, leaving the mouth and base open.

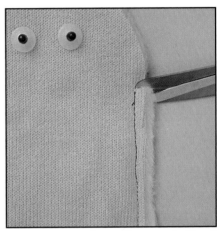

6 Cut to seam line at **B**, on each side of the body.

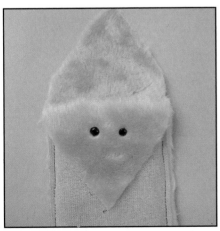

7 Fold back the head (with inserted eyes) to stitch line at **B**.

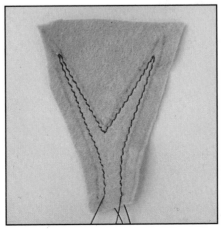

8 Stitch close to the marked line of the tongue.

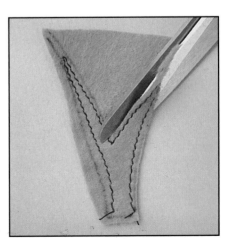

9 With sharp scissors carefully cut out the tongue shape, along the marked line.

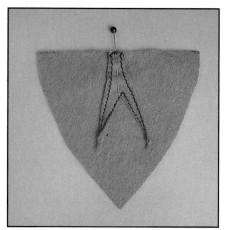

10 Pin tongue in position **A** on a felt mouth.

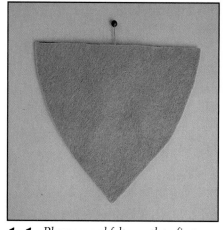

11 Place second felt mouth to first, matching **B** to **B**.

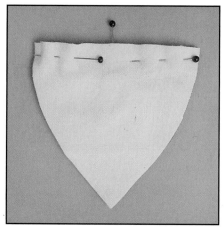

12 Then place the mouth lining on top and pin all pieces together, from **B** to **B**.

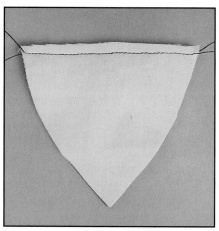

13 Stitch along seam from **B** to **B** taking care to secure the tongue at **A**.

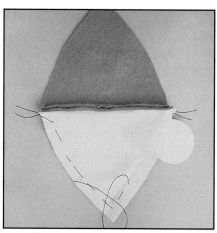

14 Unfold the mouth. Match one felt side with the lining. Tack together along one side, insert rattle then complete the tacking.

15 Turn mouth over and position rattle centrally, as shown.

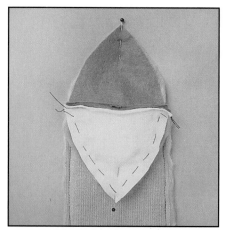

16 Turn mouth over and position onto the head and pin at **C**. The rattle should be on the same side as the inserted eyes.

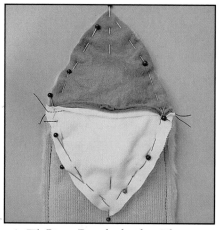

17 Pin at **B** on both sides. Then pin along each side, as shown.

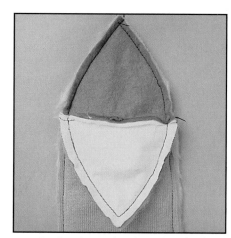

18 Stitch together from **C** to **C** along both sides. Carefully remove the tacking stitches.

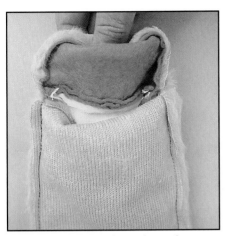

19 *Turn right side out by pushing both sides of the mouth into the body.*

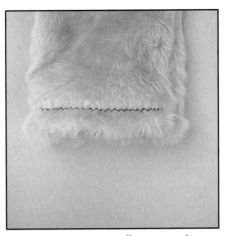

20 *Turn up seam allowance at base and neaten with zigzag stitching.*

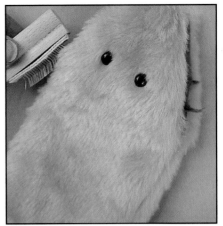

21 *With a teazle brush, brush all seams (do not brush the felt tongue and mouth).*

HOWARD *the* HAMSTER ☆

MATERIALS

○ Fawn polished fur 180mm (7″) × 160mm (6½″).

○ Beige felt 50mm (2″) × 30mm (1¼″).

○ Small piece black felt.

○ Small round nose.

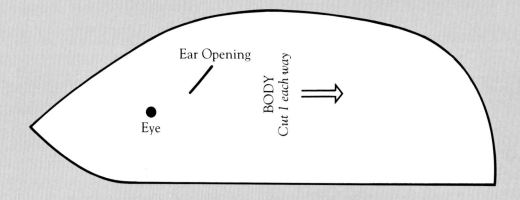

Ear Opening

● Eye

BODY
Cut 1 each way ⟹

EAR
Cut 2

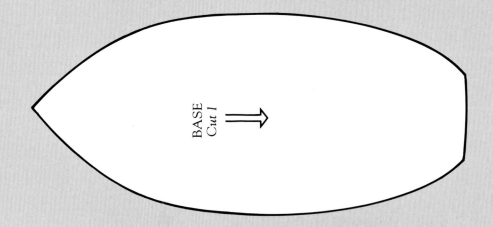

BASE
Cut 1 ⟹

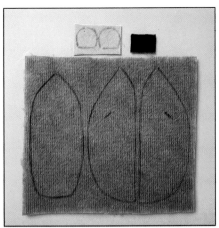

1 Make a pattern (see p.5) and draw around it on the wrong side of the fabric as shown.

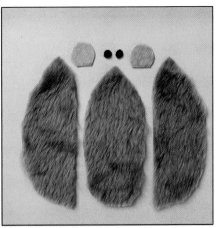

2 Cut out all pieces and check with the picture that all the sections are there.

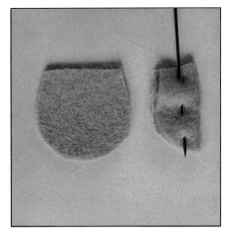

3 Pin ear in half as shown. Do not stitch.

4 Using embroidery scissors, cut ear opening on body where marked .

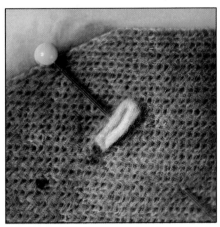

5 Place folded ear in cut with unfolded end towards the eye.

6 Fold in half, pin and stitch ear in position tapering off stitching as shown. Repeat for other ear.

7 Place two body pieces together with right sides facing. Pin top edges together.

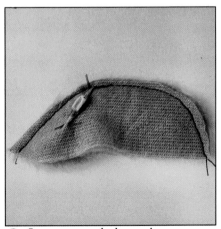

8 Sew top curved edge as shown, allowance for seams is 6mm (¼″).

9 Place top body on to base. Pin around, leaving opening on the side for stuffing.

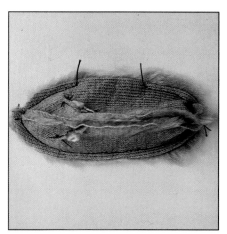

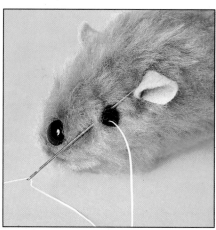

10 Carefully stitch as shown. Gently turn right side out, using fingers, and brush all seams. Make a small hole and fix nose in position of your choice.

11 Stuff carefully with sufficient stuffing to achieve a firm but not hard shape. Sew up opening with ladder stitch (see p.8). Pull up thread and secure.

12 With black thread, using small stitches and a medium size needle, sew felt eyes in place. Brush gently all over.

GILBERT *the* GUINEA PIG ☆

MATERIALS

○ Brown long haired fur (side body) 250mm (10″) × 125mm (5″).

○ White long haired fur (middle body and base) 200mm (8″) × 250mm (10″).

○ Fawn long haired fur (head) 180mm (7″) × 125mm (5″).

○ Brown felt (ears) 100mm (4″) × 405 mm (16″).

○ 2 medium round black eyes.

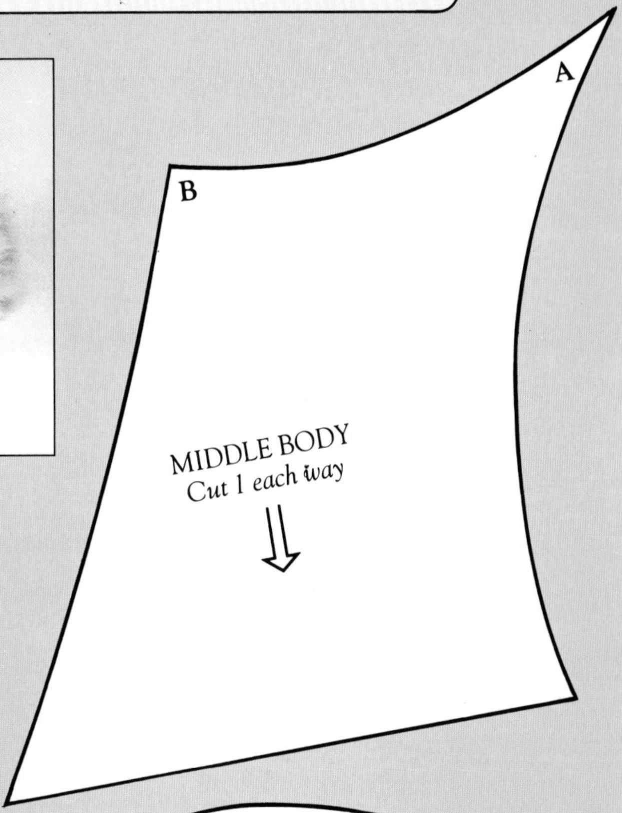

B

A

MIDDLE BODY
Cut 1 each way
⇓

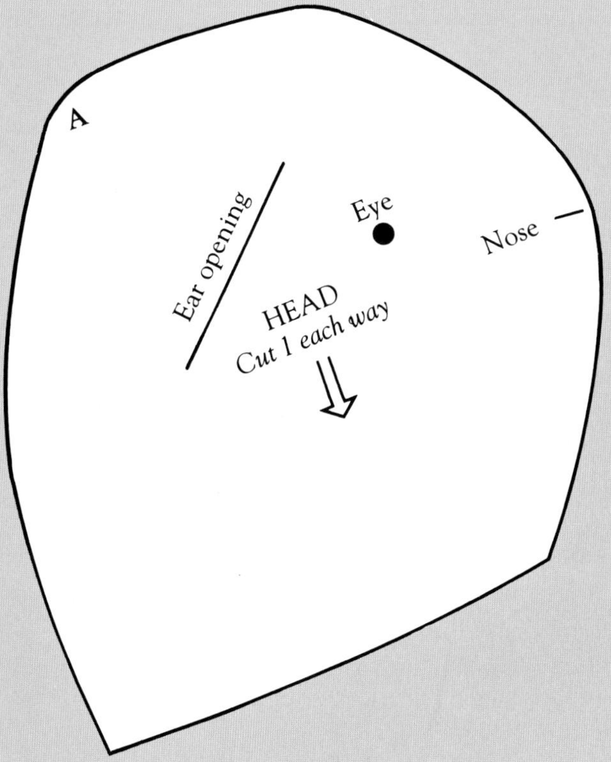

A

Ear opening

Eye ●

Nose —

HEAD
Cut 1 each way
⇓

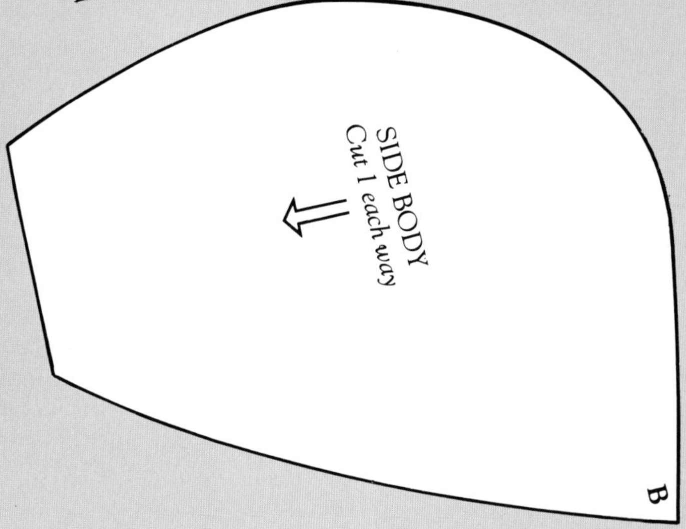

SIDE BODY
Cut 1 each way
⇐

B

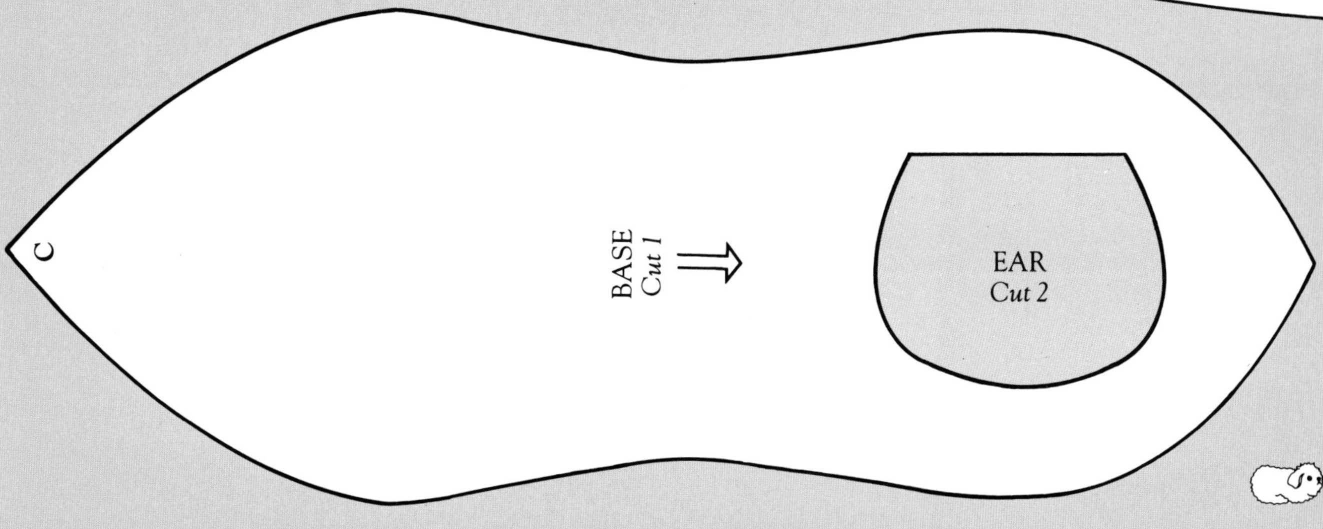

C

BASE
Cut 1
⇒

EAR
Cut 2

19

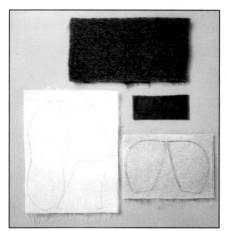

1 Make a pattern (see p.5) and draw around it on the wrong side of the fabric as shown.

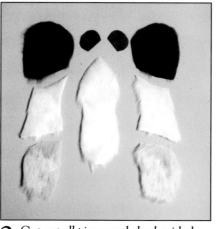

2 Cut out all pieces and check with the picture that all the sections are there.

3 Pin curved side of middle body to head, starting at **A**.

4 Stitch into place.

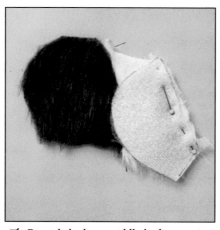

5 Pin side body to middle body, starting at **B**.

6 Stitch into place.

7 Open out body. Repeat steps *3-7* for second side.

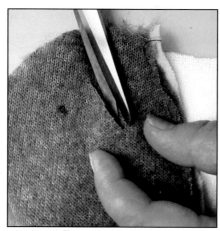

8 Carefully cut ear opening.

9 Insert straight edge of ear in the opening. Fold body over and pin into place.

10 Stitch ear in place tapering off stitching as shown. Repeat for second side.

11 Place and pin bodies together, right sides facing. Leave base open.

12 Stitch into place.

13 Pin base to body, matching, leaving a small opening as shown.

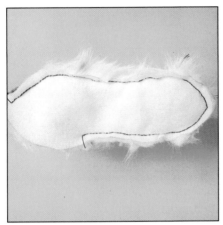

14 Stitch seam as shown.

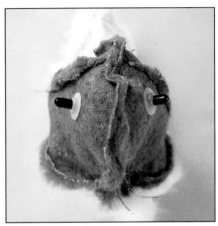

15 Insert eyes (see p.8) at points marked.

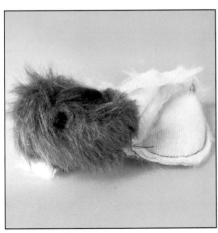

16 Gently turn right side out and brush all seams.

17 With pair of sharp scissors carefully trim a little of the long fur away from the nose.

18 Using Lazy Daisy Stitch start nose as shown.

19 Completed nose is worked from three Lazy Daisy Stitches.

20 Stuff with sufficient filling to achieve a firm, but not hard, result.

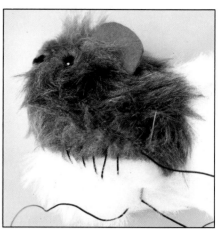

21 Sew up opening with ladder stitch (see p.8), pull up tightly and secure. Brush carefully.

HORACE the HIPPO ☆

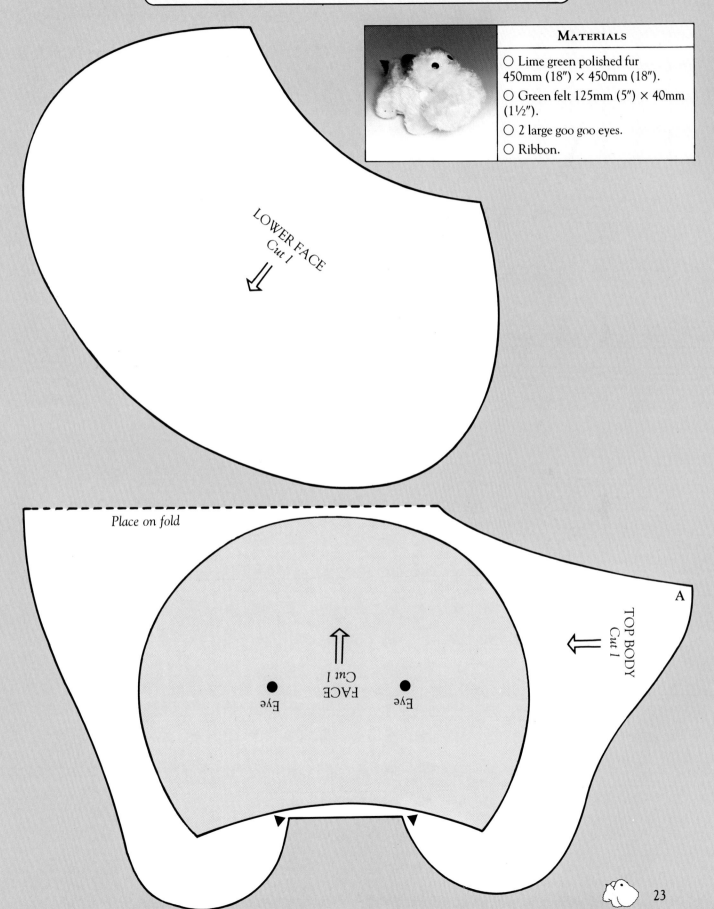

MATERIALS

○ Lime green polished fur 450mm (18") × 450mm (18").

○ Green felt 125mm (5") × 40mm (1½").

○ 2 large goo goo eyes.

○ Ribbon.

LOWER FACE
Cut 1

Place on fold

FACE
Cut 1

Eye

Eye

TOP BODY
Cut 1

A

23

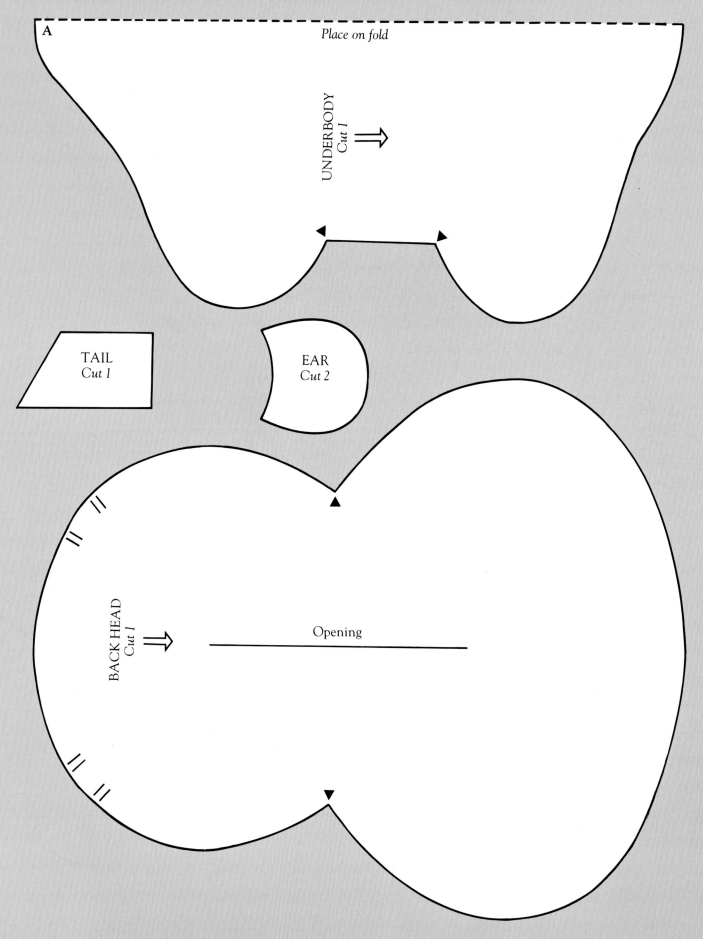

A

Place on fold

UNDERBODY
Cut 1

TAIL
Cut 1

EAR
Cut 2

BACK HEAD
Cut 1

Opening

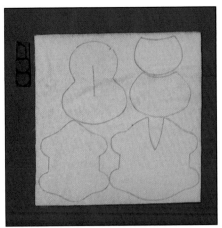

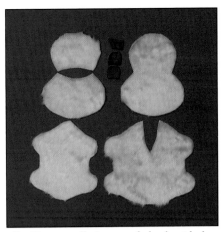

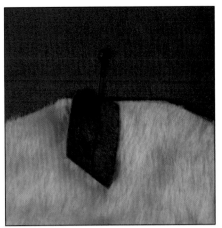

1 Make a pattern (see p.5) and draw around it on the wrong side of the fabric as shown.

2 Cut out all pieces and check with the picture that all the sections are there.

3 Pin tail to body, shorter edge outermost and longest edge to centre fold.

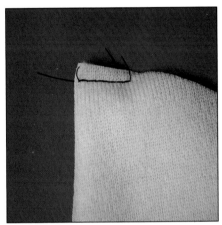

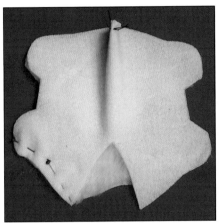

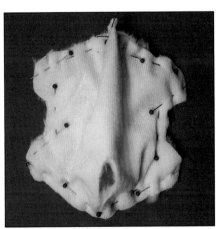

4 Fold body piece in half, then stitch in position shown. Cut to seam.

5 Unfold body piece and place onto the underbody piece, right sides facing. Pin together, matching **A**'s.

6 Carefully pin the edges, bringing top points together at **A**.

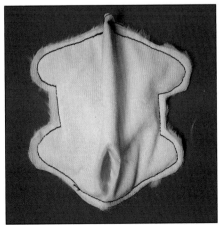

7 Stitch around edge. Cut corners to ease seams.

8 Push tail through opening to turn body right side out.

9 Brush all seams.

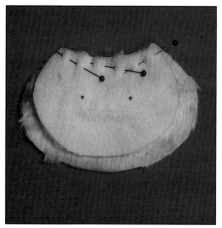

10 Place face piece on to lower face piece, right sides together. Pin as shown.

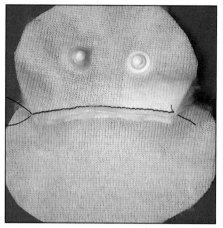

11 Stitch along seams, unfold and insert eyes (see p.8) in positions marked.

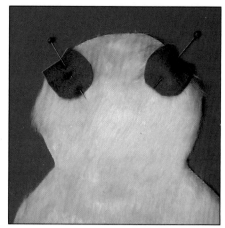

12 Pin ears on to back head piece, as indicated on template.

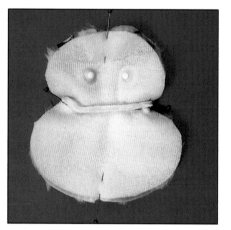

13 Place face on to head, right sides together. Pin and match at centre points.

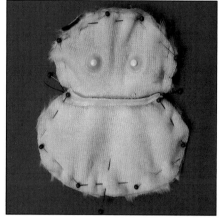

14 Pin all around outer edge.

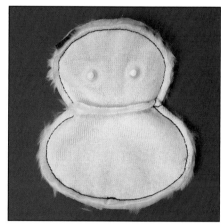

15 Stitch. Cut at corners to ease seams.

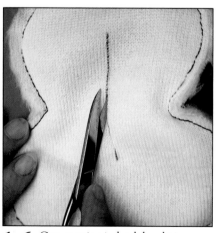

16 Cut opening in back head piece as marked on template.

17 Turn right side out.

18 Brush all seams using teazle brush.

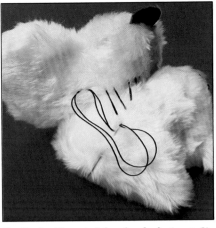

19 *Stuff with sufficient filling to achieve a firm, but not hard, shape.*

20 *Ladder stitch head to body (see p.8) matching centre back head to fold line on body. Pull up thread tightly and secure.*

21 *Fringe tail, as shown. Tie ribbon bow around neck using a double knot.*

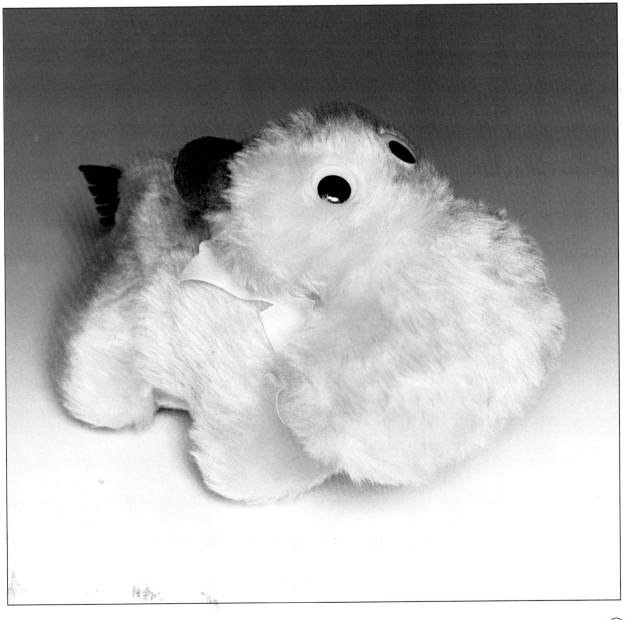

QUACKERS the DUCK ☆☆

MATERIALS

- ○ Yellow Polished Fur 385mm (15″) × 385mm (15″).
- ○ Yellow Felt 75mm (3″) × 75mm (3″).
- ○ White Lining 110mm (4½″) × 90mm (3½″).
- ○ 2 Small Goo Goo Eyes.
- ○ 1 Squeaker.

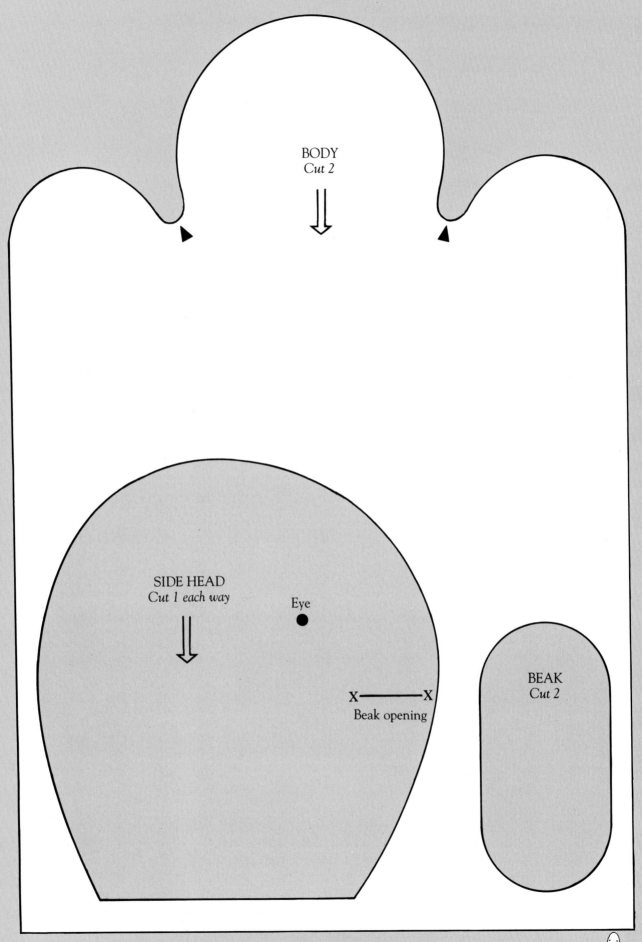

BODY
Cut 2

SIDE HEAD
Cut 1 each way

Eye

X———————X
Beak opening

BEAK
Cut 2

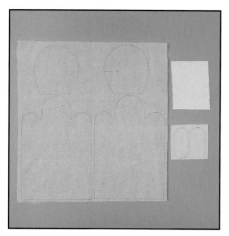

1 Make a pattern of each template shape required (see p.5). Then draw around each pattern on the wrong side of the appropriate material, as shown.

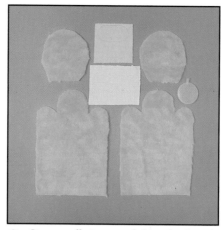

2 Cut out all pieces and then check with the picture that all the sections are there.

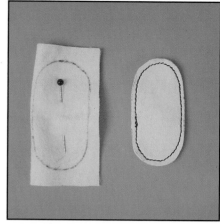

3 Fold over and pin the felt beak. Stitch just inside the marked line, then cut along the line as shown.

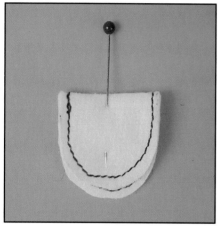

4 Fold the beak in half then position the lower beak slightly forward and pin.

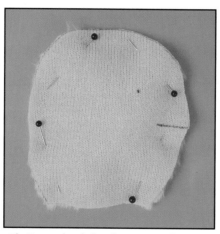

5 Pin each side head piece together around top and sides, right sides facing.

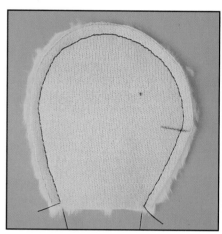

6 Stitch the two pieces together leaving the neck open.

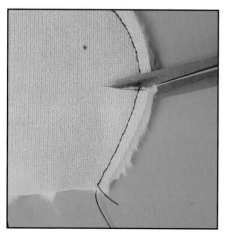

7 Cut along the beak opening, from **X** to **X**, with a pair of sharp scissors.

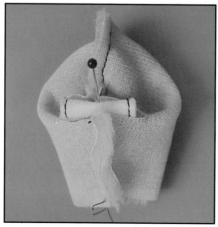

8 With the short beak uppermost, insert beak into the opening until the fold is just visible. Pin to secure.

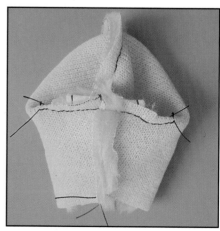

9 Carefully stitch the beak in position tapering off ends. Insert eyes (see p.8).

10 Turn the head right side out. Brush all seams.

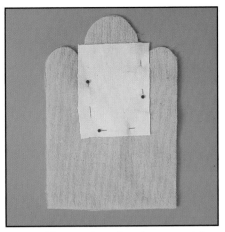

11 Place and pin the white material to the wrong side of a body piece, leave top open.

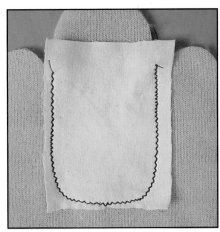

12 Stitch the material, using a zigzag stitch, leaving top open to make a pocket.

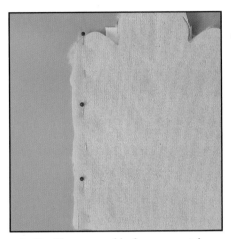

13 Place second body on top, right sides facing, and pin down left side as shown.

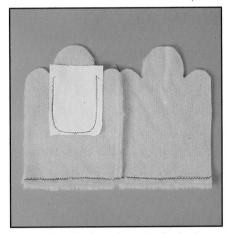

14 Stitch along the pinned side then unfold. Turn up the bottom edge and stitch into place with zigzag stitch.

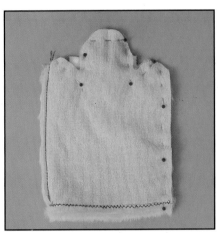

15 Fold in half and pin along top and right side as shown.

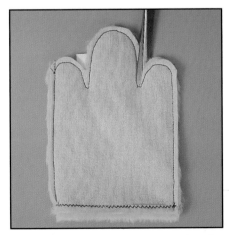

16 Stitch along the top and right side, leaving the bottom open. Carefully cut the two ease points.

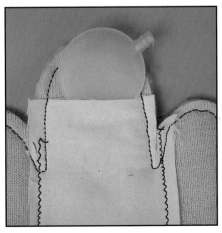

17 Slide the squeaker into the pocket until it reaches the bottom.

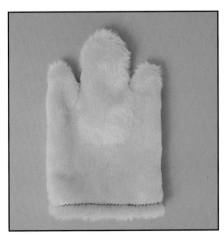

18 Turn the body right side out and brush all seams.

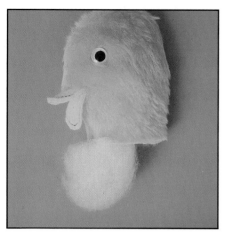

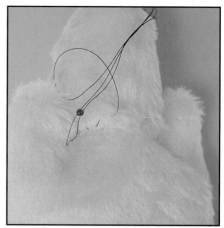

19 Insert a small amount of filling into the front side of the head.

20 Place hand into body then push the neck into the head. Ensure the squeaker is in the front.

21 Keeping neck well into the head stitch together along the neck edge with ladder stitch as shown. Brush all seams.

KERRY the KOALA ☆☆

MATERIALS

○ Polished Long Fur 510mm (20″) × 300mm (12″).

○ Lining 350mm (14″) × 125mm (5″).

○ Black Felt 180mm (7″) × 60mm (2½″).

○ 2 Teddy Eyes.

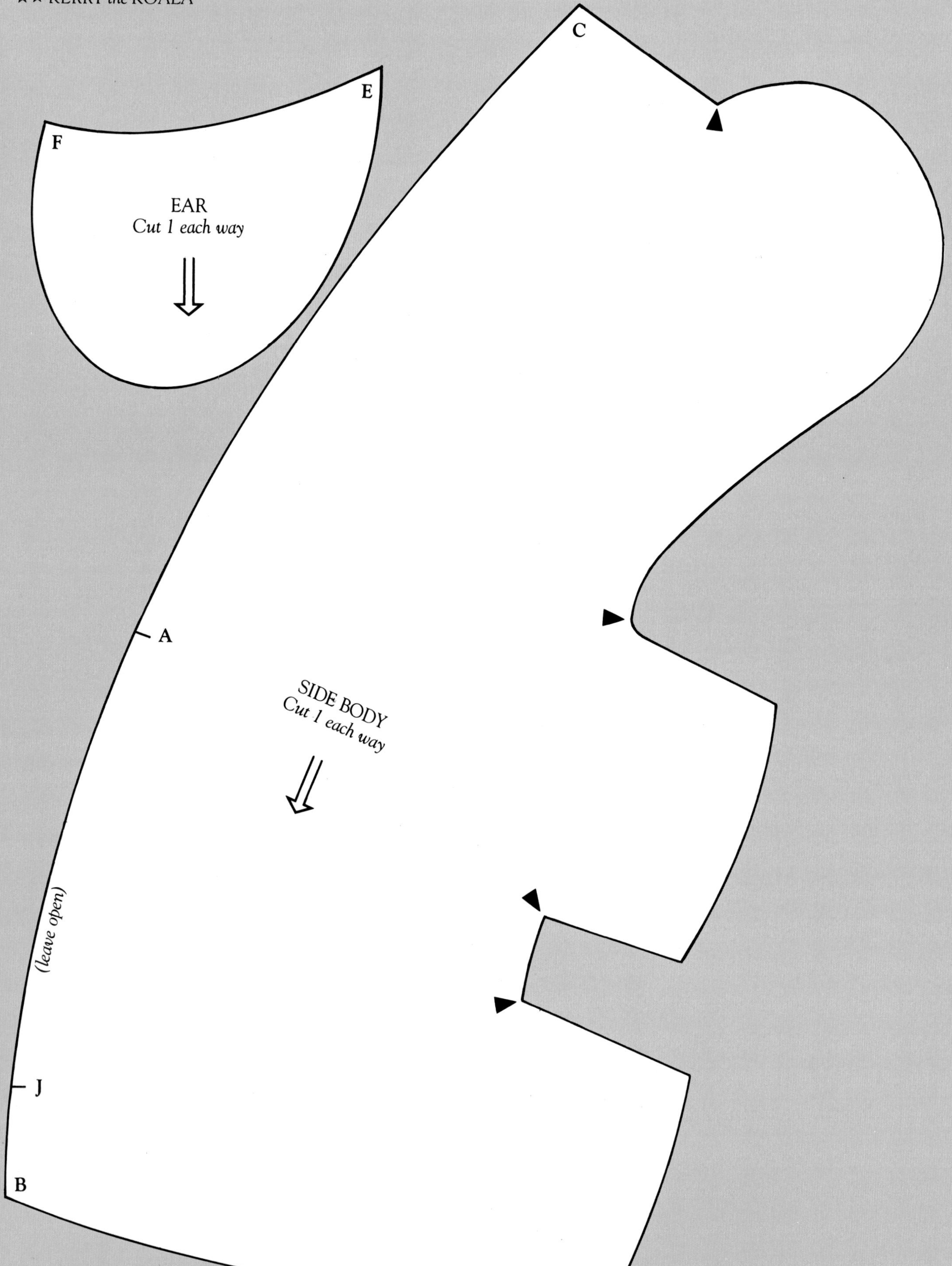

F

E

EAR
Cut 1 each way

⇓

C

A

SIDE BODY
Cut 1 each way

⇓

(leave open)

J

B

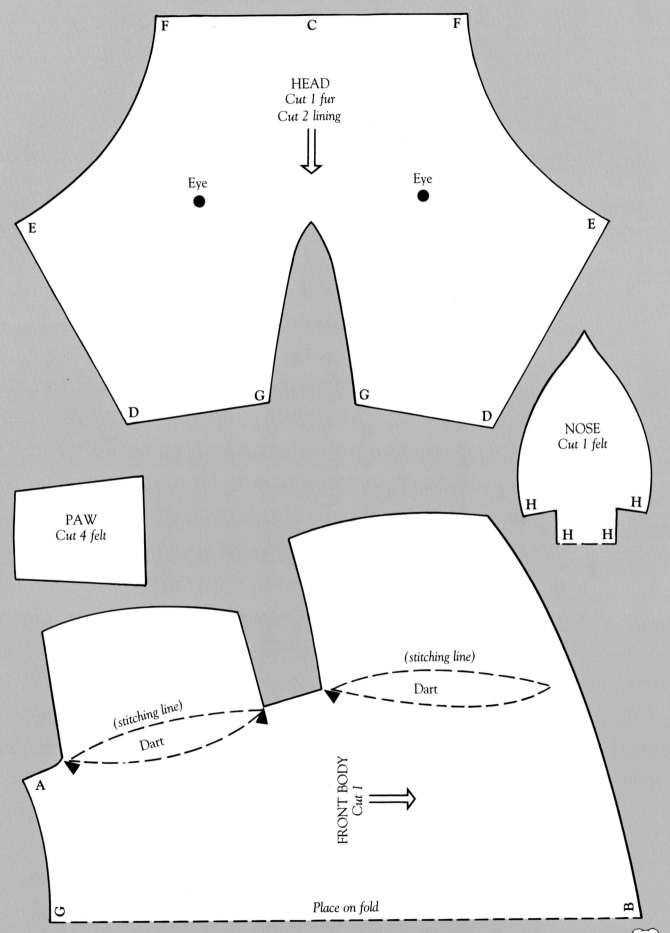

F   C   F

HEAD
Cut 1 fur
Cut 2 lining

Eye   Eye

E   E

G   G

D   D

NOSE
Cut 1 felt

H   H

H   H

PAW
Cut 4 felt

(stitching line)
Dart

(stitching line)
Dart

A

FRONT BODY
Cut 1

G   *Place on fold*   B

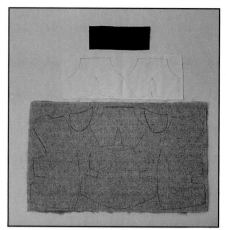

1 Make a pattern of each template shape required (see p.5). Then draw around each pattern on the wrong side of the appropriate material, as shown.

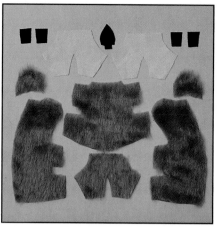

2 Cut out all pieces and check with the picture that all the sections are there.

3 Fold head in half and match **G** to **G**, then pin along seam.

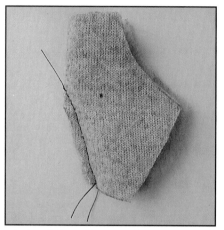

4 Stitch from **G** to top of seam tapering off, as shown. Insert eyes (see p.8).

5 Fold nose dart from **H** to **H** and pin in place.

6 Stitch the nose dart by hand, then repeat for second side.

7 Unfold to form the domed shape felt nose.

8 Place nose at dart on face. Pin left side of nose to face, then insert a small amount of filling.

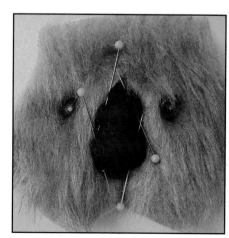

9 Shape filling in nose and pin right side, as shown.

10 *Carefully stitch nose in position by hand, using small stitches. Secure the thread.*

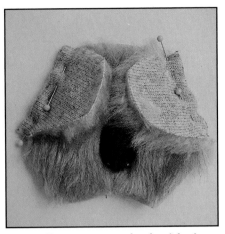

11 *Pin an ear to each side of the face matching* **E** *to* **F**.

12 *Stitch ears to face. Unfold and brush seams avoiding the felt.*

13 *Fold each limb of the body towards centre, right sides facing, to form darts then pin.*

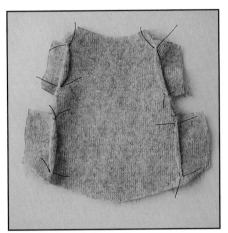

14 *Stitch each dart tapering off seam line. Unfold and brush all seams.*

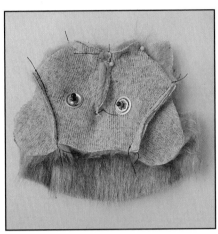

15 *Pin face to front of body, right sides facing, matching at* **D**, **G** *and second* **D**. *Stitch together.*

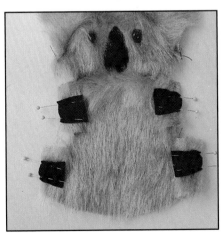

16 *Unfold front and pin short side of each paw to each limb, as shown.*

17 *Pin side bodies together, right sides facing, from* **B** *to* **J** *and* **A** *to* **C**.

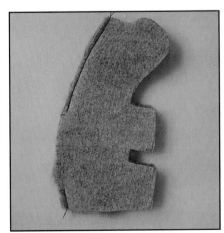

18 *Stitch together leaving seam open between* **J** *and* **A**.

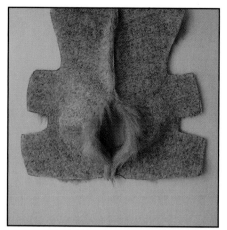

19 *Unfold back and, using the seam allowance, neaten the opening by hand sewing. Secure the thread.*

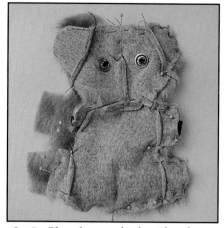

20 *Place front on back, right sides facing, matching C and B. Pin along the right side matching D at neck. Repeat on left side.*

21 *Carefully stitch around the edge of the puppet, ensuring the paws are secure in the seam line.*

22 *Cut to seam line at all the ease points.*

23 *Turn Kerry right side out by pushing the head through the opening.*

24 *With sharp scissors cut each felt paw into four pointed claws.*

25 *Brush all seams carefully avoiding the felt claws.*

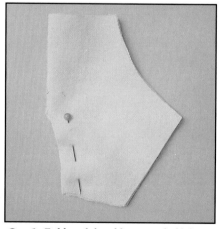

26 *Fold each head lining in half then pin and stitch from G to top of seam.*

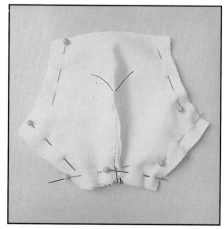

27 *Unfold, place and pin each head lining together, right sides facing, from F to D, D to D and D to F, as*

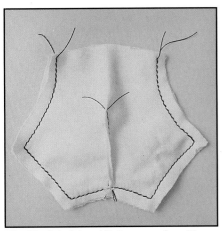

28 Stitch head linings together. Turn right side out.

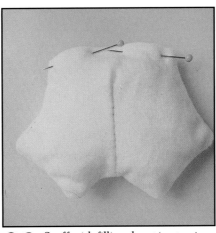

29 Stuff with filling then pin opening together. Stitch and secure.

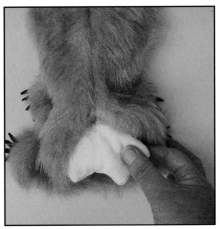

30 Slide the stuffed lining into top of head. Secure in place with a few stitches around the face.

SPOT the DALMATIAN ☆☆

MATERIALS

○ Spotty Fur 450mm (18″) × 450mm (18″).

○ Black Plush Fur 330mm (13″) × 150mm (6″).

○ 2 Medium Teddy Eyes.

○ 1 Small Round Nose.

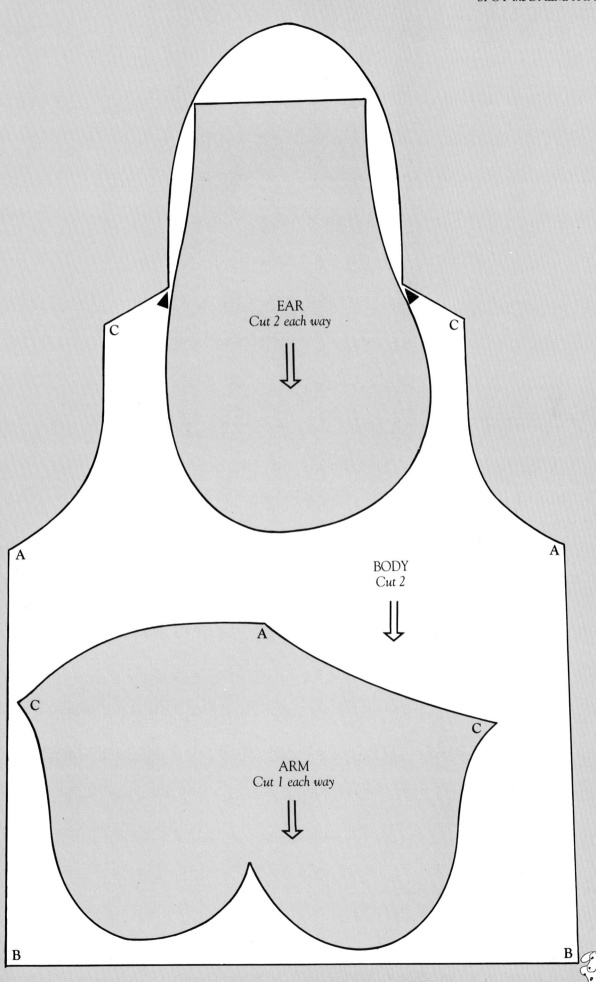

EAR
Cut 2 each way

⇓

C

C

A

A

BODY
Cut 2

⇓

A

C

C

ARM
Cut 1 each way

⇓

B

B

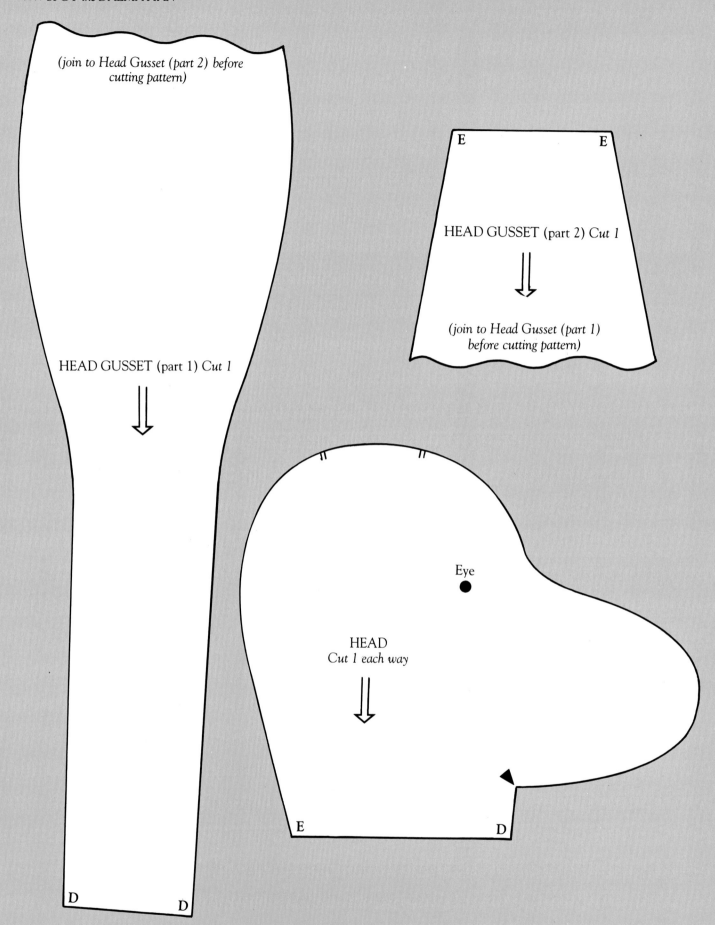

(join to Head Gusset (part 2) before cutting pattern)

HEAD GUSSET (part 1) Cut 1

E   E

HEAD GUSSET (part 2) Cut 1

⇓

(join to Head Gusset (part 1) before cutting pattern)

Eye

HEAD
Cut 1 each way

⇓

E   D

D   D

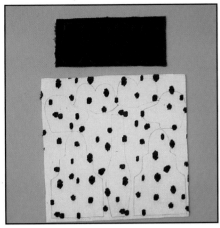

1 Make a pattern of each template shape required (see p.5). Then draw around each pattern on the wrong side of the appropriate material, as shown.

2 Cut out all pieces and then check with the picture that all the sections are there.

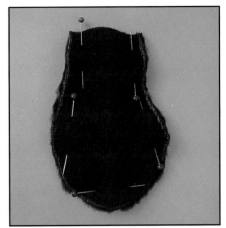

3 Pin a pair of ears together, right sides facing, leaving short side open.

4 Stitch around ears as shown leaving top open.

5 Turn right side out using the blunt end of a pencil. Brush seam.

6 Pin ear to top of head as shown. Repeat steps 3-6 for second side.

7 Pin head gusset to head, right sides facing, from E to D.

8 Carefully stitch gusset to head.

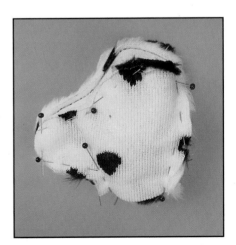

9 Pin second side to head gusset, right sides facing, from D to E. Leave neck open.

43

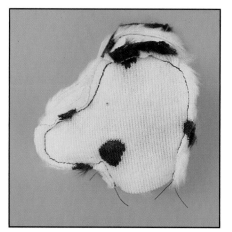

10 Stitch from **E** to **D** as shown. Insert eyes (*see p.8*).

11 Carefully turn head right side out. Brush all seams. Insert nose (*see p.8*).

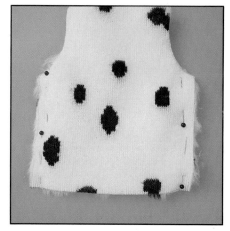

12 Position body sides together, right sides facing, and pin from **A** to **B** on both sides.

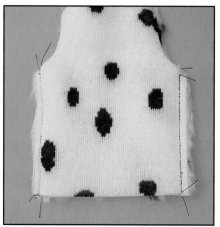

13 Stitch along each side from **B** to **A** as shown.

14 Fold back top half of body and pin on arm, matching at **C**, **A** and **C**. Repeat for second arm.

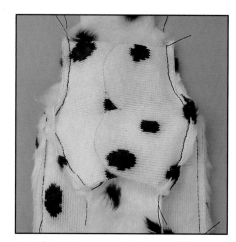

15 Stitch arms to body carefully as shown.

16 Open arms out. Refold puppet and pin from the top of the arms to **C**, over the top to second **C**, then to the top of the arm.

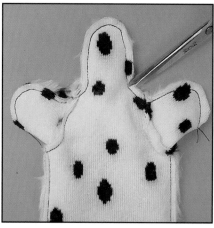

17 Stitch from arm to arm following the stitching line across the top. Cut at ease points as shown.

18 Turn right side out and brush all seams. Using the seam allowance, neaten the bottom with zigzag stitch.

19 Stuff the muzzle and front of head firmly to fill out the face.

20 Place hand in puppet, slide head over top of body positioning as required.

21 Pin head in place and, using seam allowance, sew head to body firmly with ladder stitch.

LAURA the LAMB ☆ ☆

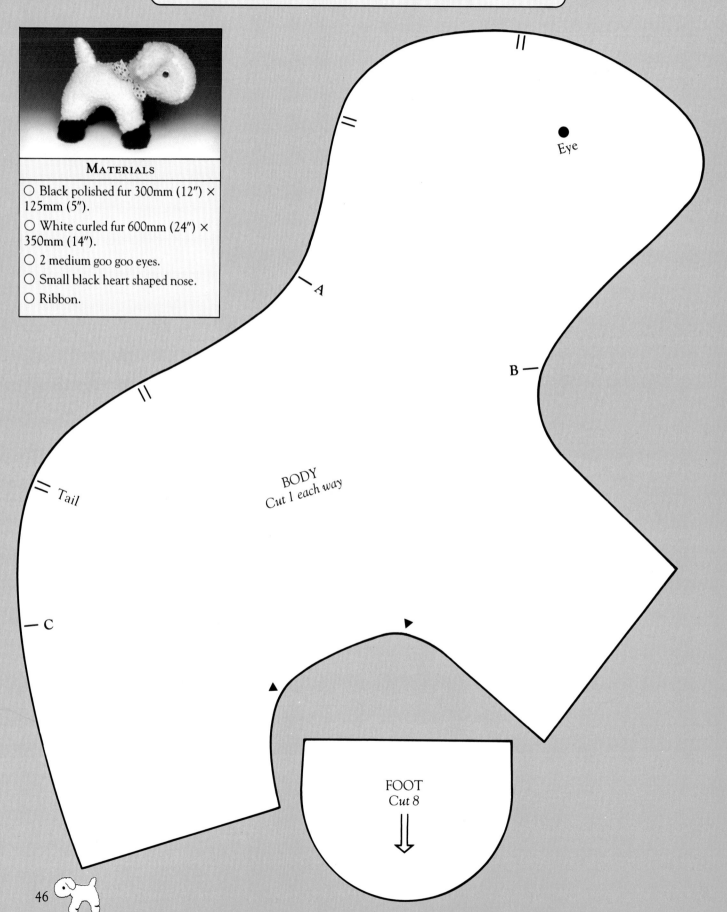

MATERIALS

○ Black polished fur 300mm (12") × 125mm (5").

○ White curled fur 600mm (24") × 350mm (14").

○ 2 medium goo goo eyes.

○ Small black heart shaped nose.

○ Ribbon.

Eye

A

B

Tail

C

BODY
Cut 1 each way

FOOT
Cut 8

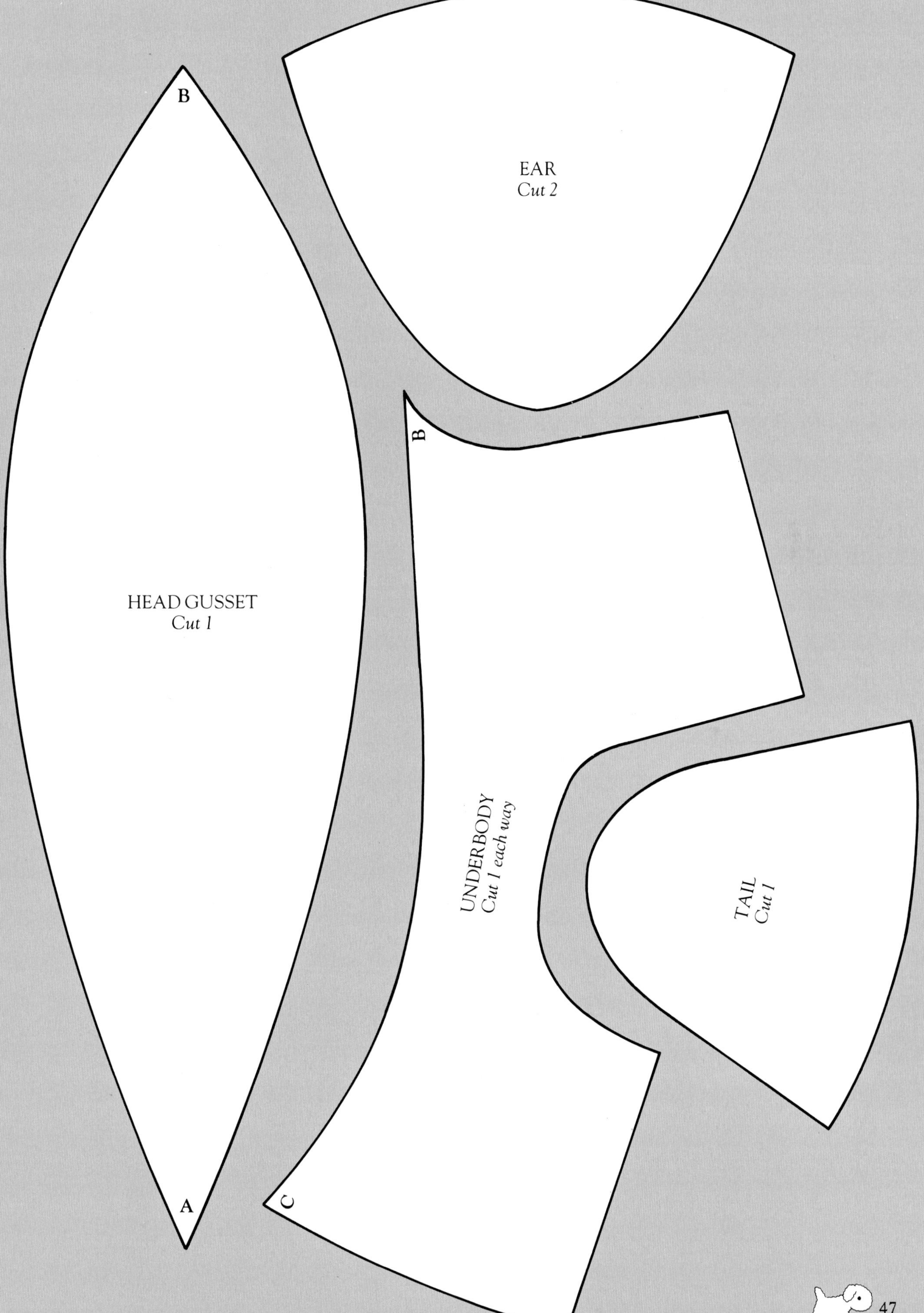

B

EAR
Cut 2

B

HEAD GUSSET
Cut 1

UNDERBODY
Cut 1 each way

TAIL
Cut 1

A

C

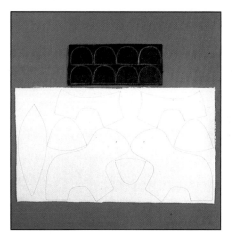

1 Make a pattern (see p.5) and draw around it on the wrong side of the fabric as shown.

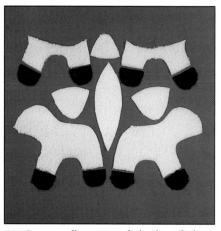

2 Cut out all pieces and check with the picture that all the sections are there.

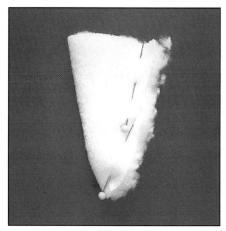

3 Fold ears in half and pin.

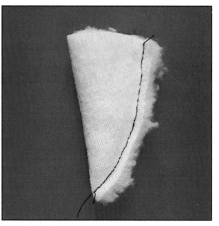

4 Stitch ears as shown.

5 Turn right side out. Do not brush. Repeat steps *3*, *4* & *5* for the other ear and the tail.

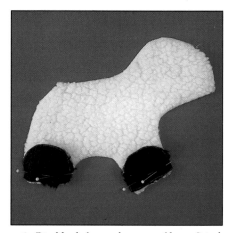

6 Pin black feet to bottom of legs. Stitch feet to legs.

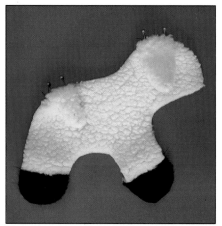

7 With right side facing, pin ears and tail in place as shown.

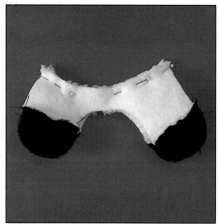

8 Match underbody, right side facing. Pin top edge, leaving an opening in the middle as shown.

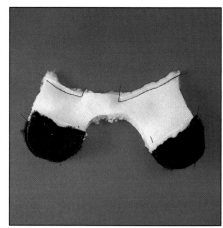

9 Stitch seam as shown.

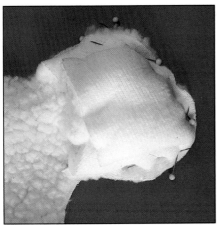

10 Place head gusset. Starting at back of neck at **A**, work round the top of the head to nose and continue under muzzle to **B**.

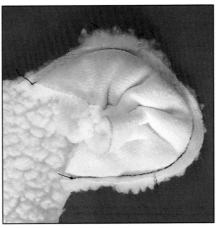

11 Stitch round head as shown.

12 Place second side on top of first side, right sides facing. Pin from **C** over head to **B**.

13 Stitch around body as shown.

14 Carefully snip seam at **B** and **C**.

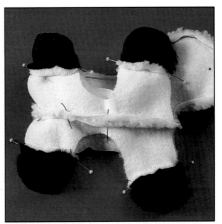

15 Open up legs. Place underbody on top, right sides together, and carefully pin feet in place as shown.

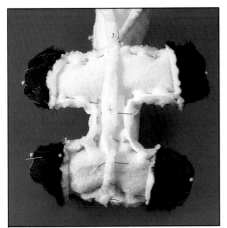

16 Pin round underbody.

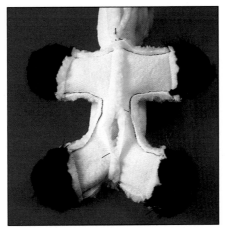

17 Stitch carefully as shown. Insert eyes (see p.8).

18 Turn right side out by pushing the head, then legs, into centre of body and easing through the opening. Insert nose (see p.8).

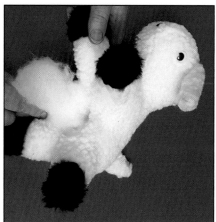

19 *Stuff carefully to achieve a firm but not hard shape. Begin with legs, using a stuffing tool if necessary, then the head, and finally the body.*

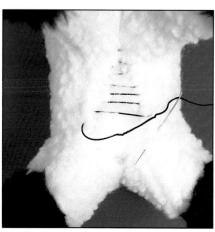

20 *Close opening with ladder stitch (see p.8). Pull thread up tightly and secure.*

21 *Brush feet only. Tie bow round neck.*

BOBO the RABBIT ☆☆

MATERIALS

○ Blue polished fur
360mm (14½") × 265mm (10½").

○ White polished fur
135mm (5½") × 135mm (5½").

○ 2 small goo goo eyes.

○ Small heart shaped nose.

○ Ribbon.

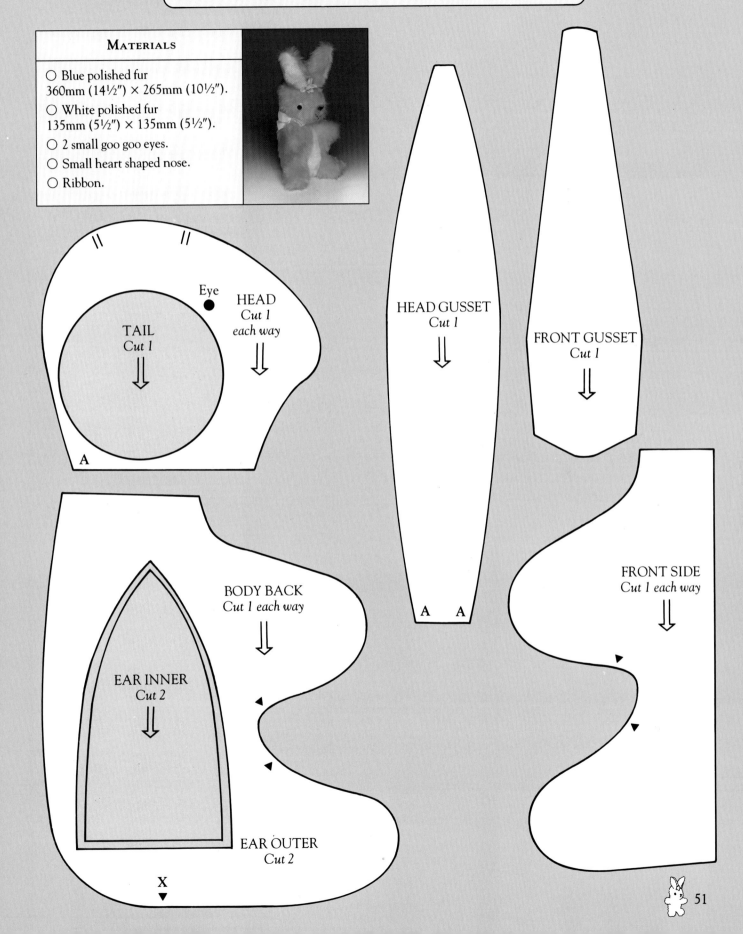

TAIL
Cut 1

Eye

HEAD
Cut 1
each way

A

HEAD GUSSET
Cut 1

FRONT GUSSET
Cut 1

BODY BACK
Cut 1 each way

EAR INNER
Cut 2

EAR OUTER
Cut 2

X

A   A

FRONT SIDE
Cut 1 each way

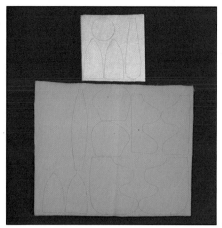

1 Make a pattern (see p.5) and draw around it on the wrong side of the fabric as shown.

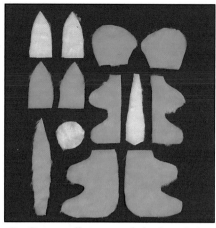

2 Cut out all pieces and check with the picture that all the sections are there.

3 Pin together inner and outer ears with right sides of material facing.

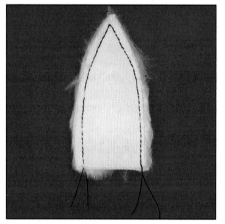

4 Stitch the two pieces together leaving base open.

5 Carefully turn the ear through to the right side. Push out top with blunt end of pencil.

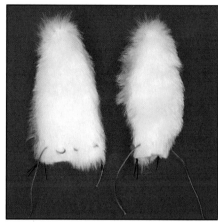

6 Sew a gathering thread along base of each ear, draw up and secure.

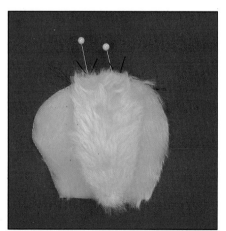

7 Pin an ear to each side of head piece with white side to right side of head. Tack.

8 Pin head gusset to side of head starting from back of neck at mark **A**.

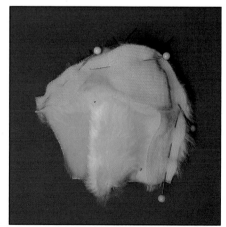

9 Continue pinning gusset to head finishing at nose.

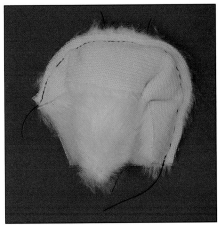

10 Stitch pieces together, as shown.

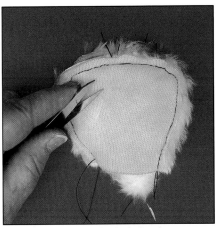

11 Stitch second side to head gusset. Insert eyes (see p.8).

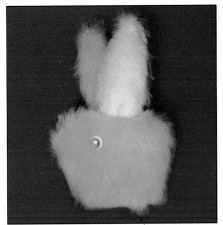

12 Gently turn head to right side, easing seams at curves. Brush seams.

13 Insert nose (see p.8). Embroider mouth with stranded cotton (see p.8).

14 Stuff head firmly and sew gathering thread around base.

15 Draw up thread leaving a small opening as shown. Fasten off end firmly.

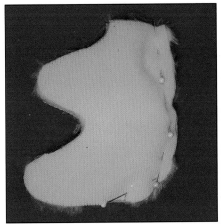

16 Pin top edge of body-back together to X with right sides facing.

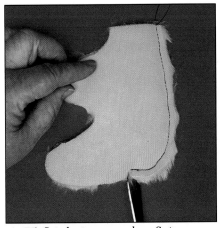

17 Stitch pieces together. Snip to seam line at X, taking care not to cut stitches.

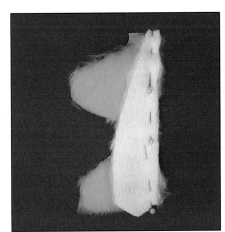

18 Pin front gusset to one of the side front pieces.

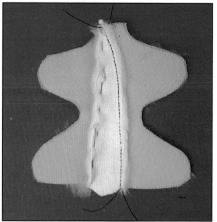

19 Stitch together. Pin second side to gusset and stitch.

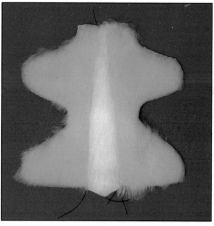

20 Open out and brush seams.

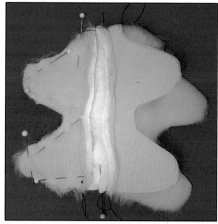

21 Place front on back with right sides together. Pin front top shoulder towards tail as shown. Repeat for second side.

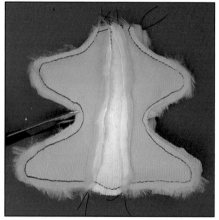

22 Stitch as shown leaving top open. Snip to seam line on curves taking care not to cut stitching.

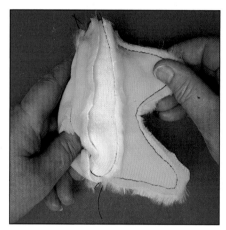

23 Push each limb into centre of body and turn right side out.

24 Ease the top of each limb out with the blunt end of a pencil.

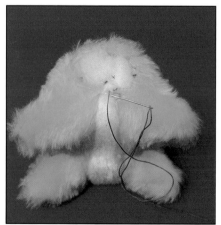

25 Stuff limbs and then body with sufficient filling to achieve a firm but not hard result. Run gathering thread around neck, pull up leaving small opening, and secure.

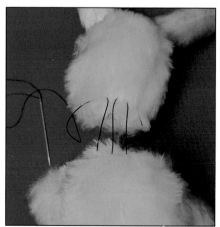

26 Matching head centre back to body centre back, stitch head to body using ladder stitch (see p.8). Pull thread up tightly and secure.

27 Brush all over gently. Finish with ribbon tied around neck in double knot and bow.

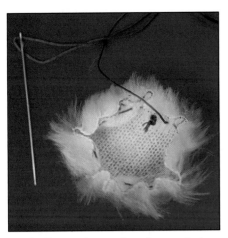

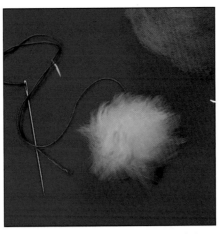

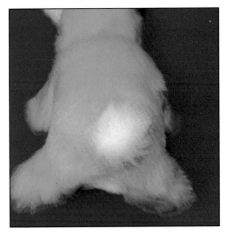

28 Run gathering thread around edge of tail piece, draw up slightly.

29 Stuff tail, draw thread up tightly and secure.

30 Stitch tail to body with ladder stitching. Draw up tightly and secure. Brush all seams.

TIBBLES the CAT ☆☆

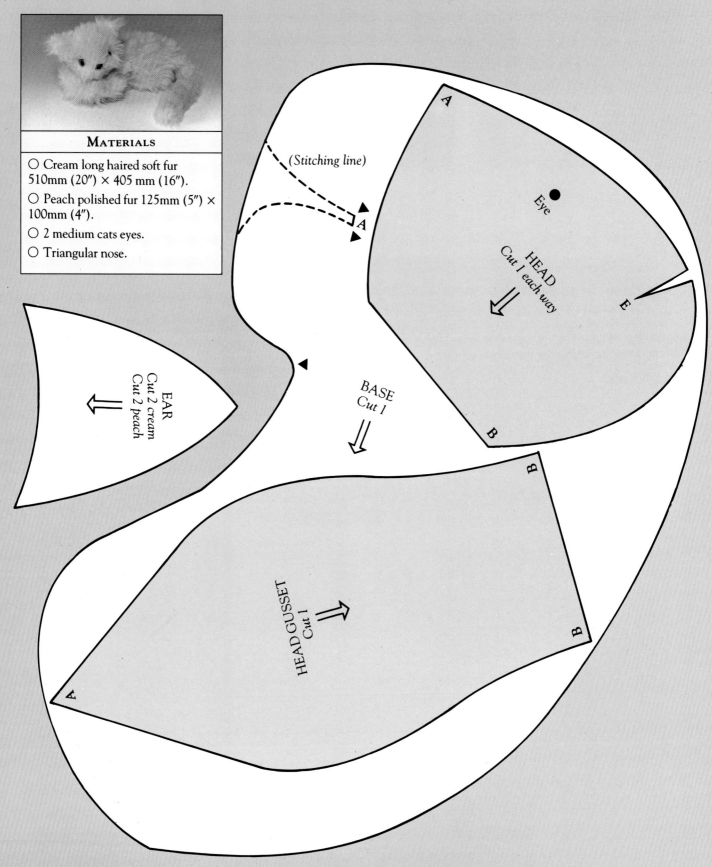

(Stitching line)

A

A

Eye

HEAD
Cut 1 each way

E

B

EAR
Cut 2 cream
Cut 2 peach

BASE
Cut 1

B

HEAD GUSSET
Cut 1

B

A

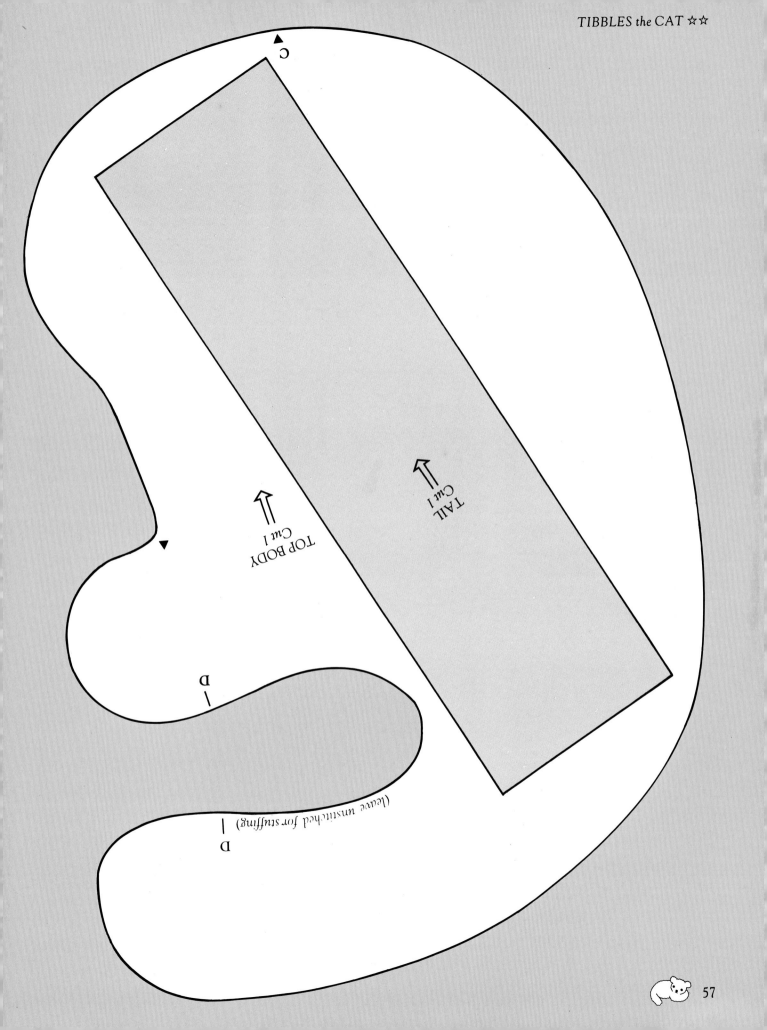

▲ C

TAIL
Cut 1

TOP BODY
Cut 1

▲

D

D
(leave unstitched for stuffing)

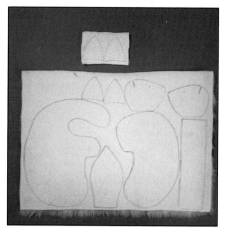

1 Make a pattern (see p.5) and draw around it on the wrong side of the fabric as shown.

2 Cut out all pieces and check with the picture that all the sections are there.

3 Pin inner ear to outer ear, right sides facing together, and stitch as shown. Turn right side out and brush the seam. Repeat for second ear.

4 Pin side head to gusset matching **A**'s and **B**'s.

5 Carefully stitch as shown.

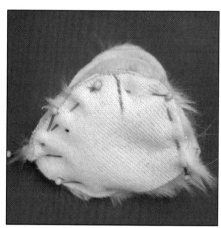

6 Place second head on gusset, right sides together and pin in place starting at **B** and finishing at neck.

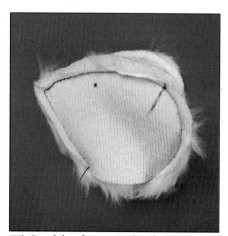

7 Stitch head gusset to head, leaving neck open.

8 Cut from mark **E** at bottom of ear line on side of head over the top to **E** mark on second side of head as shown.

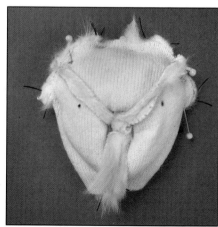

9 Pin ears in opening as shown, keeping inner ear towards the front.

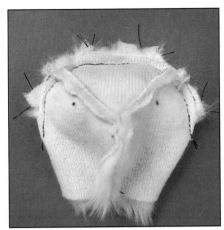

10 Sew ears into place tapering off stitching at each side. Insert eyes at mark (see p.8).

11 Turn right side out and insert nose (see p.8). Brush seams carefully. Stuff head with sufficient filling to achieve a firm, but not hard, result.

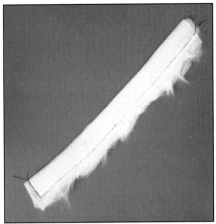

12 Fold tail lengthways, right sides facing, and pin. Stitch as shown leaving one end open.

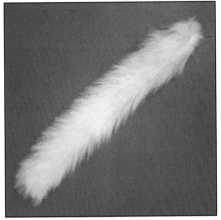

13 Turn tail right side out using the blunt end of a knitting needle. Brush seam and tail gently to release trapped fur.

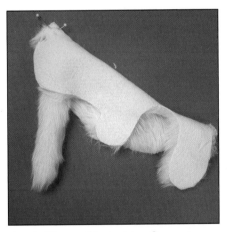

14 Place tail in position **C** on top body. Fold body over as shown and pin carefully at **C**.

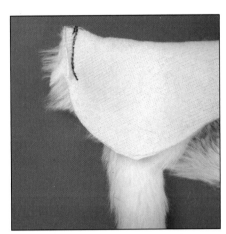

15 Stitch tail into position as shown. Snip to seam end.

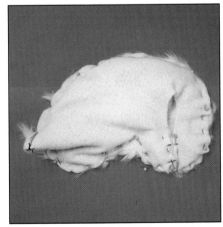

16 Place top body on to base, right sides facing, and starting at **D** pin top body to base finishing at second **D**.

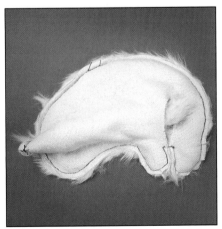

17 Carefully stitch top body to base.

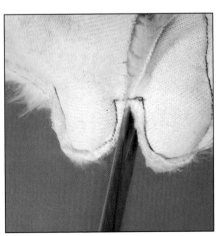

18 Carefully snip between paws at **D** to stitching line as shown.

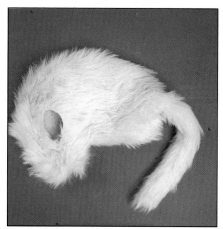

19 Turn right side out and brush all seams.

20 Stuff body using sufficient filling to achieve a firm, but not hard, result (work stuffing into the paws with fingers).

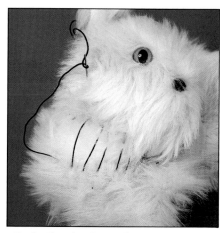

21 Place head in a chosen position on neck and secure with ladder stitch (see p.8). Pull thread up tightly and secure. Brush gently and finish with a bow.

OLIVER the OWL ☆☆

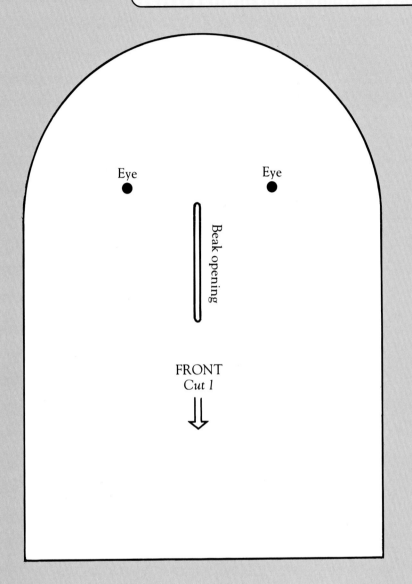

Eye ●   Eye ●

Beak opening

FRONT
Cut 1
⇓

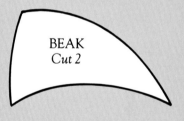

MATERIALS

○ Brown polished fur
460mm (18") × 230mm (9").

○ White polished fur
125mm (5") × 180mm (7").

○ 2 pieces orange felt 75mm (3") ×
100mm (4").

○ 2 large teddy eyes.

BEAK
Cut 2

FOOT
Cut 4

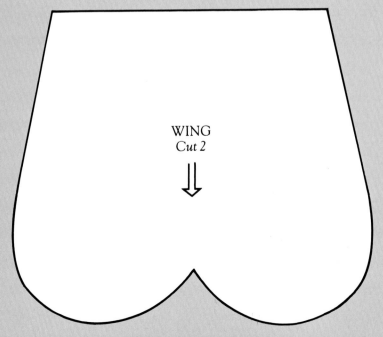

WING
Cut 2
⇓

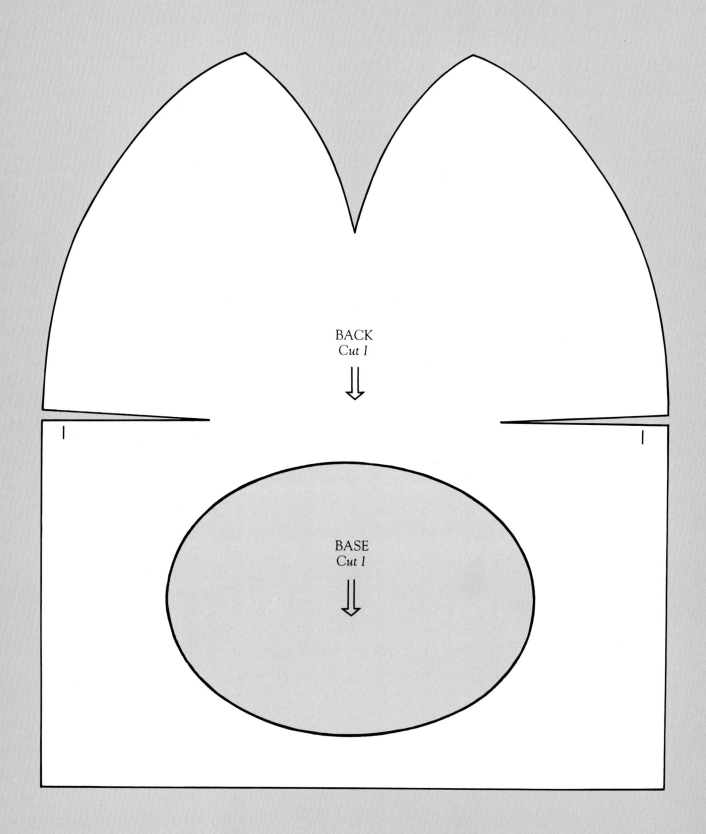

BACK
Cut 1
⇓

BASE
Cut 1
⇓

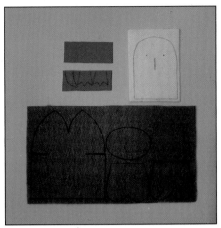

1 Make a pattern (see p.5) and draw around it on the wrong side of the fabric as shown.

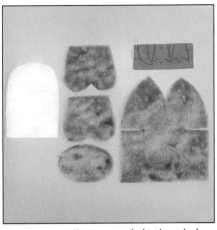

2 Cut out all pieces and check with the picture that all the sections are there.

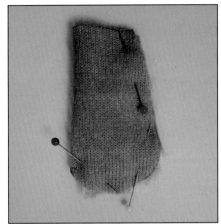

3 Fold and pin each wing with right side of material together.

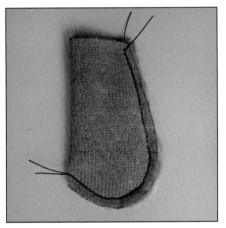

4 Stitch along edges leaving top opening as shown. Repeat steps *3-4* for second ear.

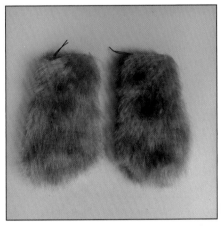

5 Turn wings right side out and brush seams.

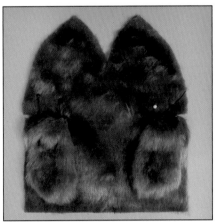

6 Place and pin each wing 6mm (¼") in from side edge of body.

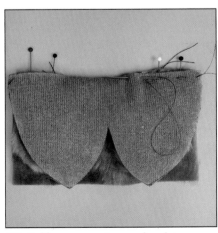

7 Fold top over wings and tack in position as shown.

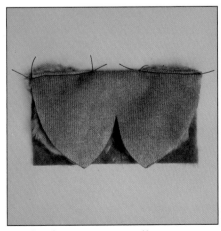

8 Stitch seam tapering off at centre as shown.

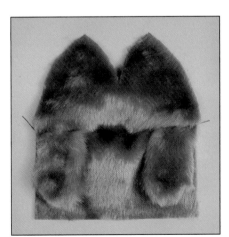

9 Unfold and brush seams.

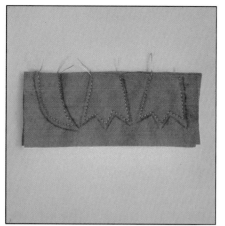

10 *Pin felt pieces together. Stitch feet and beak just inside marked line, leaving tops open as shown.*

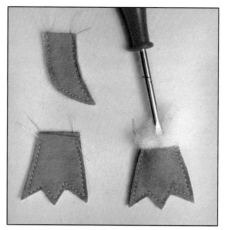

11 *Cut out each piece and stuff lightly.*

12 *Pin beak at centre opening on front.*

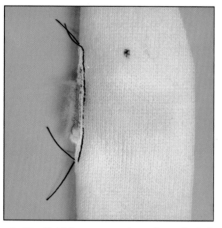

13 *Fold front over, then pin and stitch beak in position tapering off ends as shown.*

14 *Insert eyes (see p.8).*

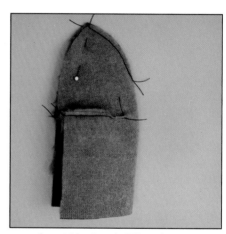

15 *Fold back in half lengthways, pin and stitch top dart tapering off end.*

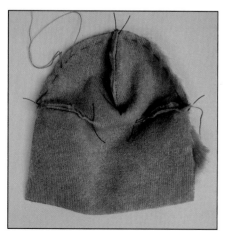

16 *Unfold back. Run gathering thread from top of right wing to top of left wing.*

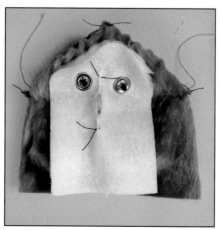

17 *Draw up gathering thread slightly. Place front on back, right sides together, as shown.*

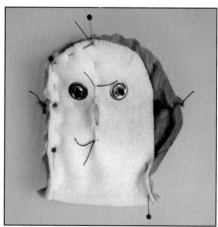

18 *Pin top centre and bottom corners.*

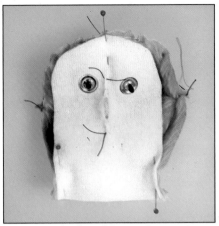

19 Pin back and front sides together, ensuring back fits evenly to front.

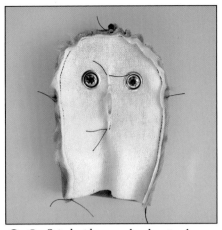

20 Stitch sides together leaving bottom open.

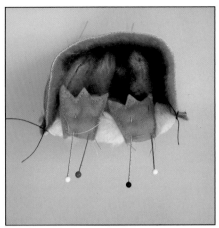

21 Pin feet to bottom front as shown.

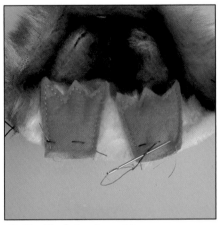

22 Tack feet in position.

23 Pin base to bottom of body leaving centre back opening.

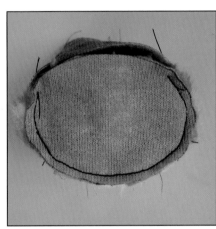

24 Stitch base as shown.

25 Push head through gap at base.

26 Gently turn right side out.

27 Brush all seams.

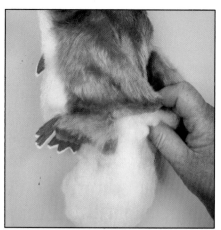

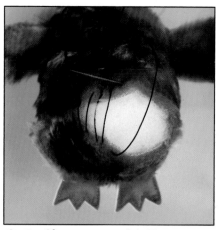

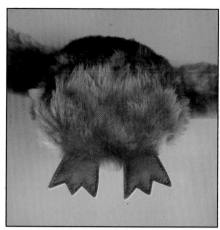

28 Stuff with sufficient filling to achieve a firm but not hard result.

29 Close opening with ladder stitch (see p.8). Pull up thread tightly and secure.

30 Brush all over.

DILLY the DUCK ☆☆☆

MATERIALS

○ Dark yellow polished fur 330mm (13″) × 450mm (18″).

○ Pale yellow medium pile fur 350mm (14″) × 120mm (5″).

○ 2 pieces of grey felt 120mm (5″) × 85mm (3½″).

○ 2 small pieces of orange and yellow felt.

○ 2 small teddy eyes.

○ Dotted pattern cotton material 230mm (9″) × 150mm (6″).

○ Length of broderie anglaise.

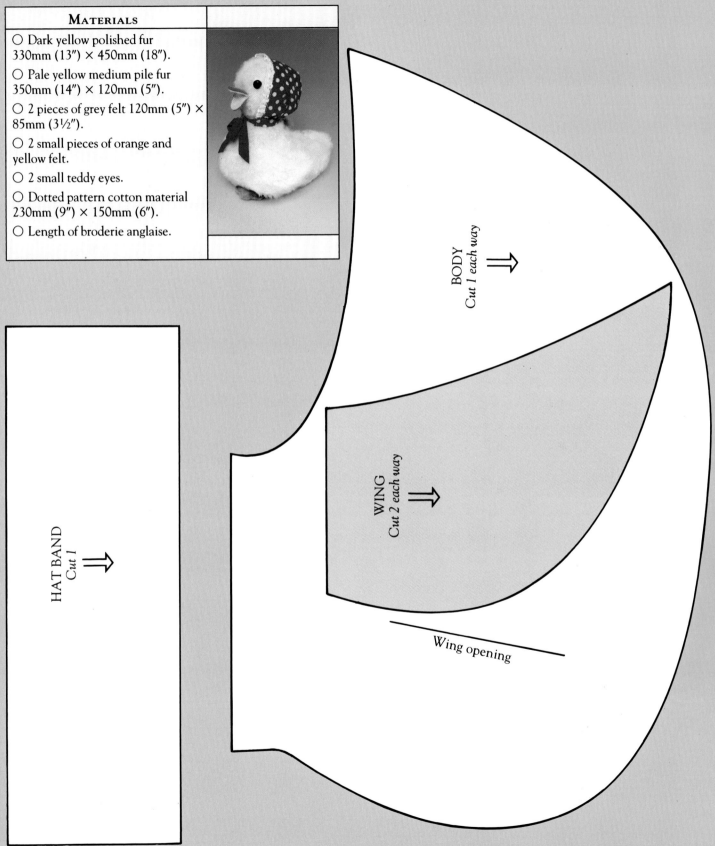

BODY
Cut 1 each way ⟹

WING
Cut 2 each way ⟹

Wing opening

HAT BAND
Cut 1 ⟹

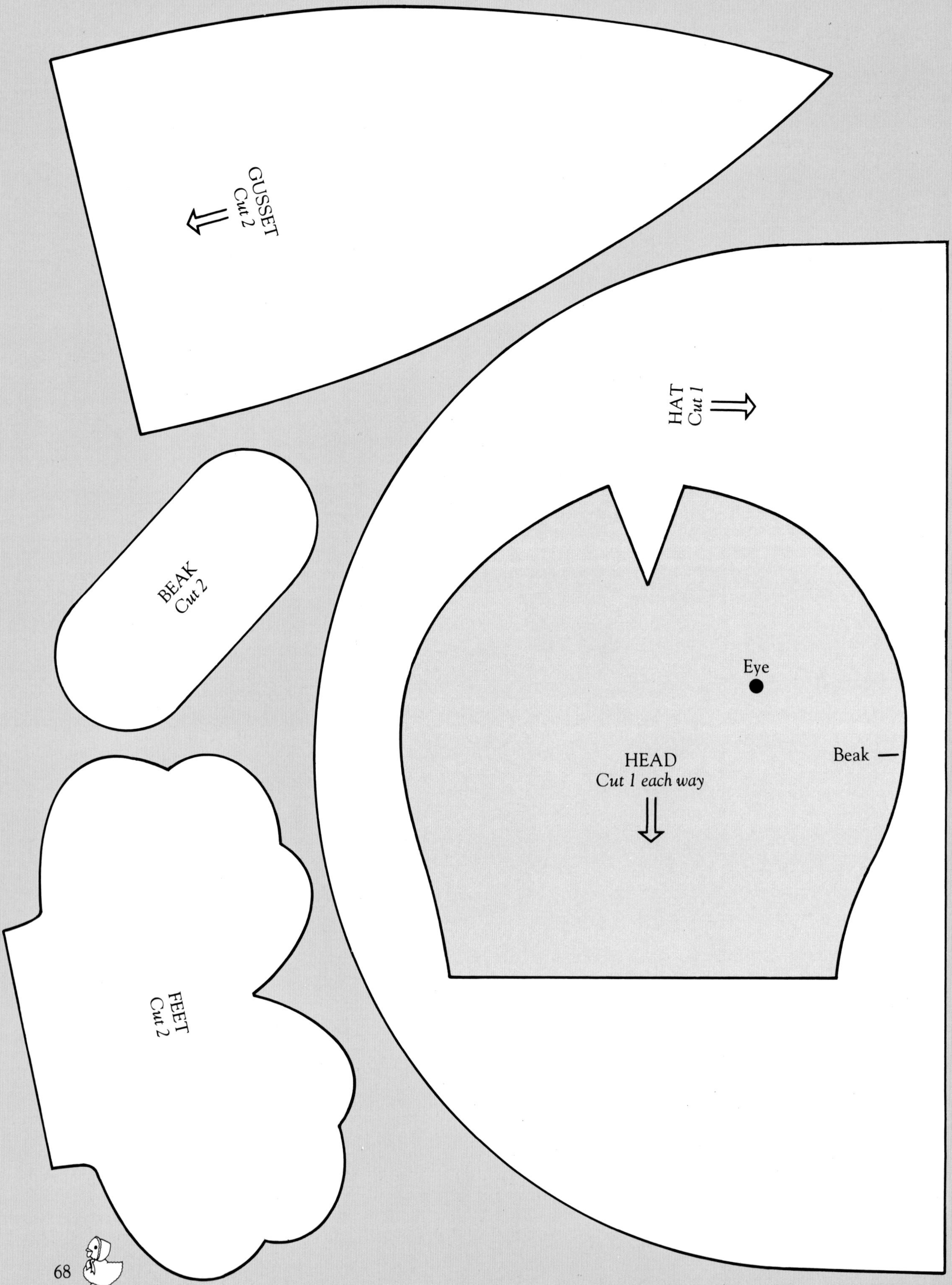

GUSSET
Cut 2

HAT
Cut 1

BEAK
Cut 2

FEET
Cut 2

Eye

HEAD
Cut 1 each way

Beak —

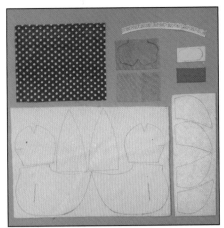

1 Make a pattern (see p.5) and draw around it on the wrong side of the fabric as shown.

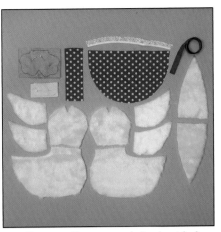

2 Cut out all pieces and check with the picture that all the sections are there.

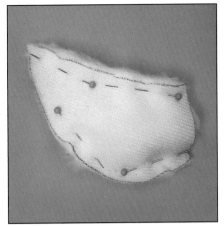

3 Pin wings together with right sides facing leaving short side open.

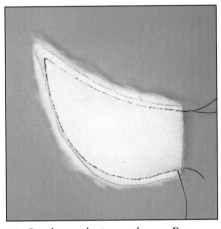

4 Stitch round wing as shown. Repeat for second wing.

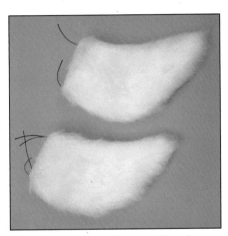

5 Turn wings inside out and brush seams.

6 Pin and stitch darts on each head piece, tapering end.

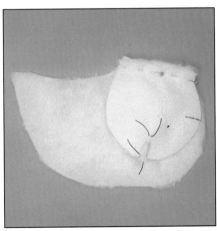

7 Pin each head piece to each body piece and stitch in position.

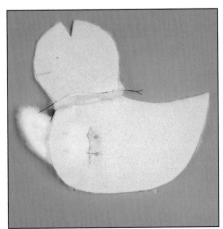

8 Open out each side of body. Cut openings for wings. Place wing inside opening and pin in place as shown.

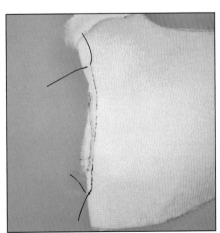

9 Fold each body piece over, pin and stitch wing tapering off ends as shown.

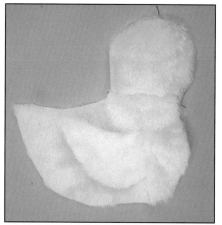

10 Unfold each piece and brush seams.

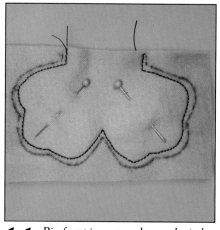

11 Pin feet pieces together and stitch inside marked line.

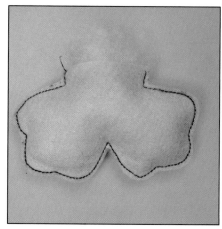

12 Cut along line and stuff lightly.

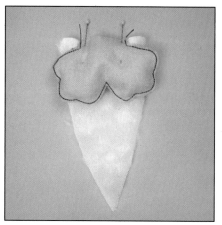

13 Pin feet to straight edge of gusset.

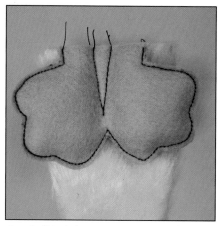

14 Stitch feet to gusset in 'V' shape as shown.

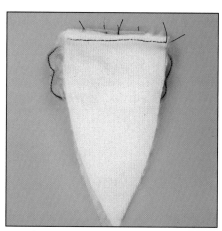

15 Place second gusset on top of first, with right sides together. Pin and stitch.

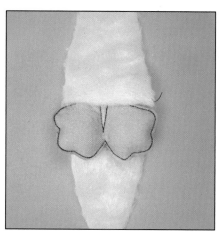

16 Open out and brush seams.

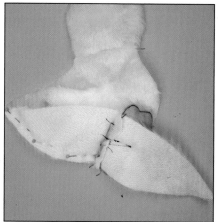

17 With right sides facing, starting at tail, place and pin gusset to body (ensuring feet are facing forward).

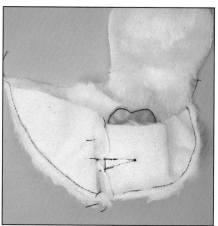

18 Stitch gusset to body, taking care not to trap feet in seam.

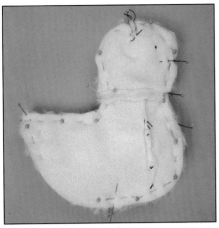

19 Pin second side of body on to first, leaving opening behind feet as shown.

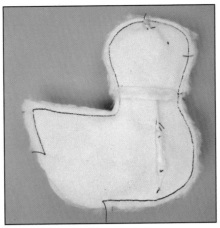

20 Stitch round edge.

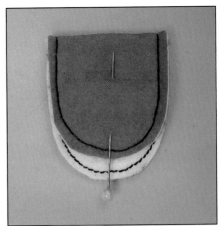

21 Stitch beak pieces together just inside line. Cut out. Fold in half and pin.

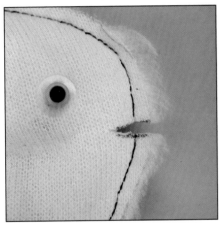

22 Insert eyes (see p.8). Cut opening for beak.

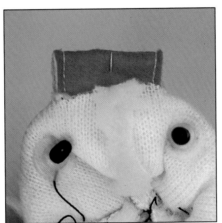

23 Push open end of beak through opening and pin.

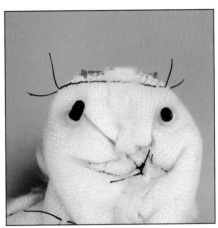

24 Pin fold edge to cut edges and stitch carefully together, tapering off ends.

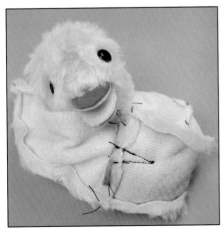

25 Turn right side out.

26 Brush all seams.

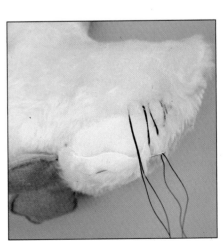

27 Stuff with sufficient filling to achieve a firm result. Close opening with ladder stitch (see p.8). Pull thread up tightly and secure. Brush all over.

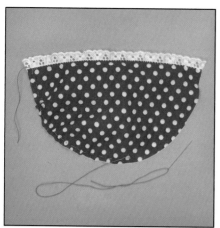

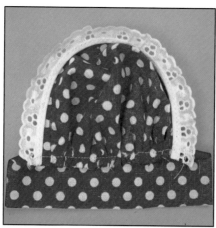

28 Fold under turning on straight edge of hat. Stitch on lace. Run a gathering thread around curved edge.

29 Draw up gathering thread to fit length of band as shown. Stitch together.

30 Fold over band to enclose the ribbon. Hand stitch together to complete the hat.

POLLY the PARROT ☆☆

MATERIALS

○ Red polished fur 200mm (8″) × 230mm (9″).
○ Yellow polished fur 100mm (4″) × 125mm (5″).
○ Blue polished fur 60mm (2½″) × 150mm (6″).
○ Black polished fur 100mm (4″) × 150mm (6″).
○ Red felt 100mm (4″) × 85mm (3½″).
○ Black felt 60mm (2½″) × 85mm (3½″).
○ Ribbon.
○ 2 small teddy eyes.

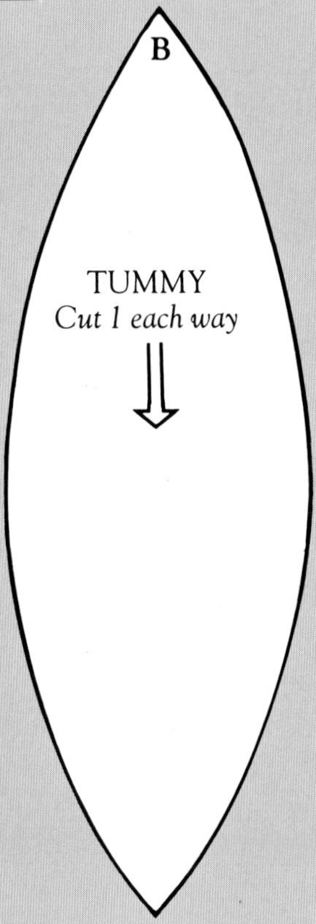

B

TUMMY
Cut 1 each way
⇓

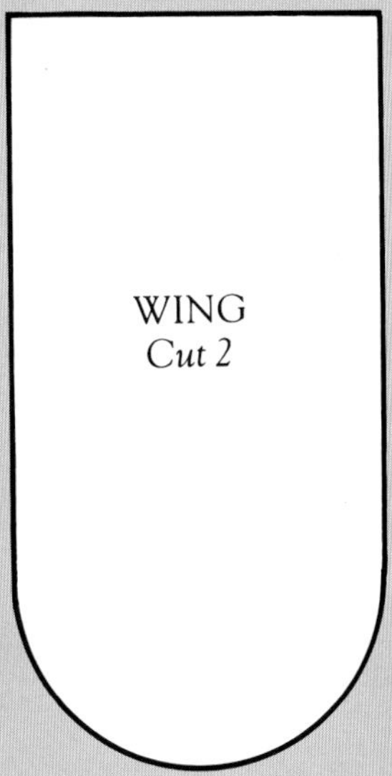

WING
Cut 2

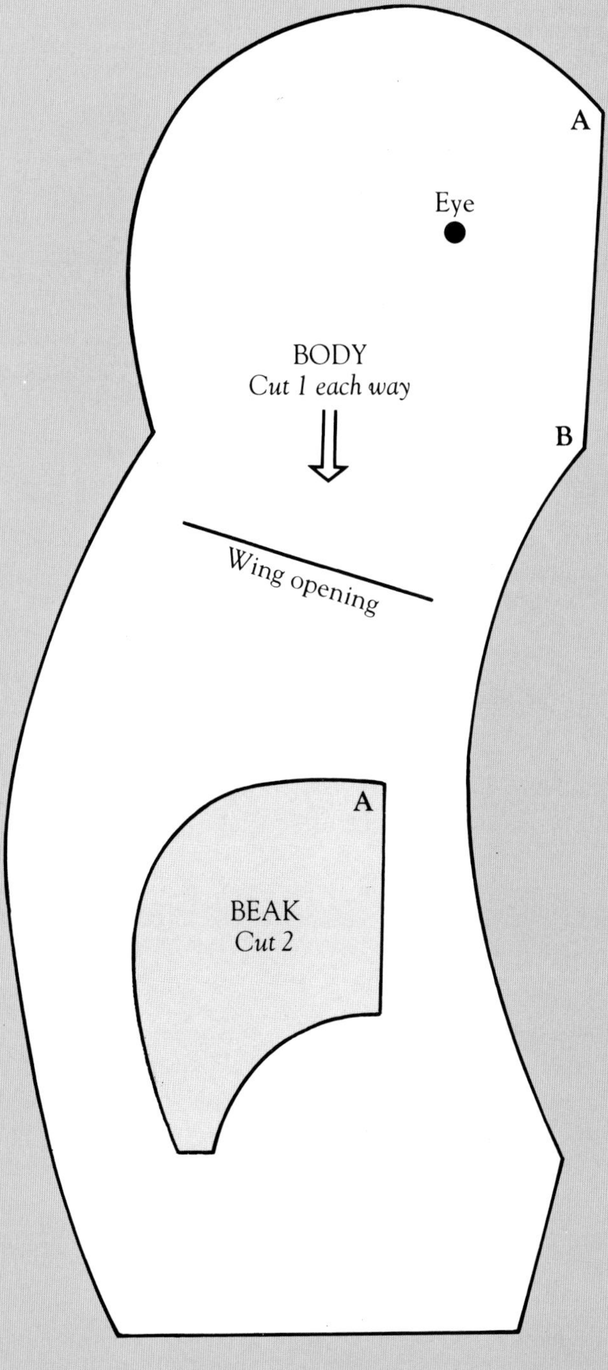

A

Eye

BODY
Cut 1 each way
⇓

B

Wing opening

A

BEAK
Cut 2

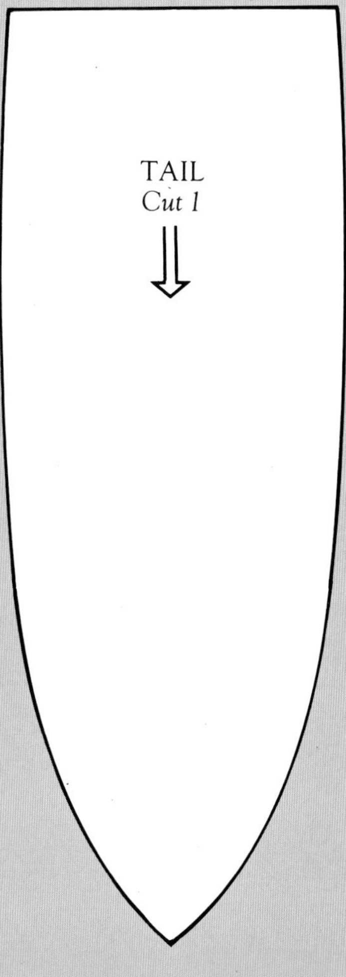

TAIL
Cut 1
⇓

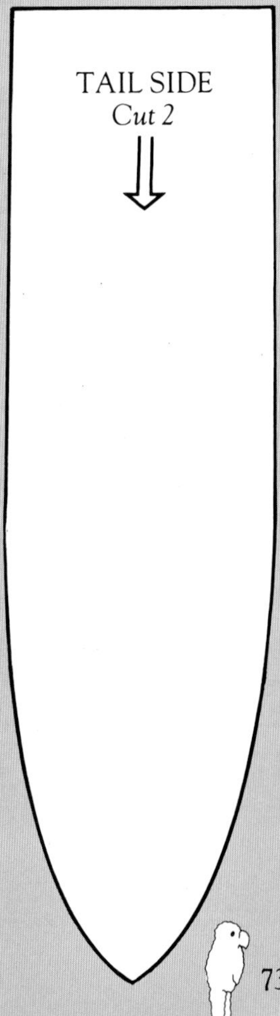

TAIL SIDE
Cut 2
⇓

73

1 Make a pattern (see p.5) and draw around it on the wrong side of the fabric as shown.

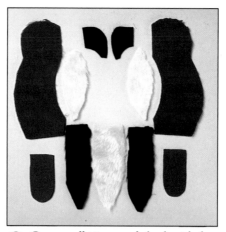

2 Cut out all pieces and check with the picture that all the sections are there.

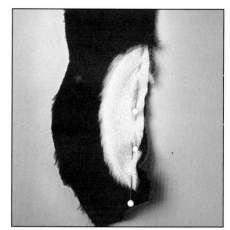

3 Place tummy on body, right sides together, matching at **B**. Pin as shown.

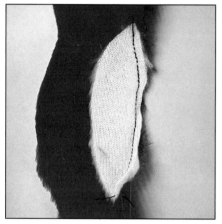

4 Stitch tummy into place.

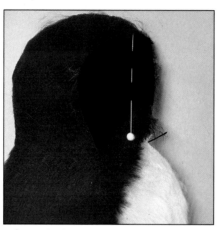

5 Pin beak to head, matching at **A** and stitch into place.

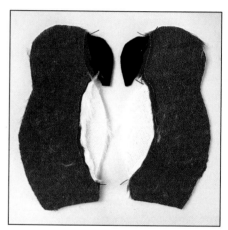

6 Repeat steps **3-5** for second side. Open out and brush fur seams.

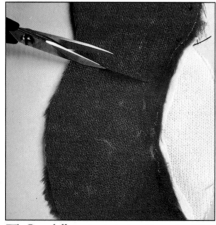

7 Carefully cut wing opening at position indicated.

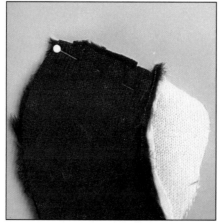

8 Insert top of wing into opening. Fold over body and pin into place.

9 Stitch wing in place tapering off ends as shown.

10 Unfold. Repeat steps *7-9* for second side.

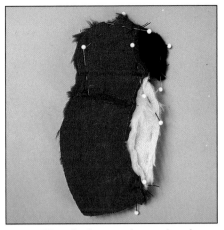

11 Place bodies together, right sides facing. Pin from back of head, across the top of the head, round the beak, and down the tummy.

12 Stitch into place. Insert eyes in position marked (see p.8).

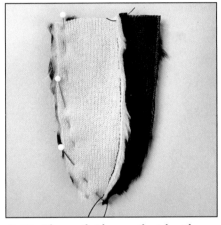

13 Place tail side on tail, right sides together. Pin and stitch first side. Open out. Pin second side as shown and stitch. Open out. Brush seams.

14 Place tail on body, right sides facing. Pin into place.

15 Stitch tail to body. Unfold. Brush seam.

16 Fold body in half. Pin from bottom of tail to top of body, leaving an opening for stuffing just below the neck.

17 Stitch as shown.

18 Turn right side out. Brush all fur seams. Stuff with sufficient filling to achieve a firm, but not hard, result.

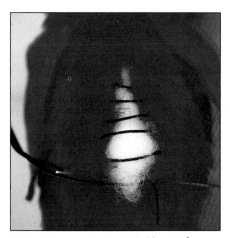

19 *Close opening with ladder stitch (see p.8). Pull thread up firmly and secure.*

20 *Pin ribbon to top of head as shown. Secure with small stitches.*

21 *Tie ends into a bow and form hanging loop.*

TEDDY *the* GLOVE PUPPET ☆☆

MATERIALS

○ Gold Plush Fur 510mm × 355mm (20″ × 14″)
○ Honey Plush Fur 205mm × 150mm (8″ × 6″)
○ 2 Medium Teddy Eyes
○ 1 Small Animal Nose

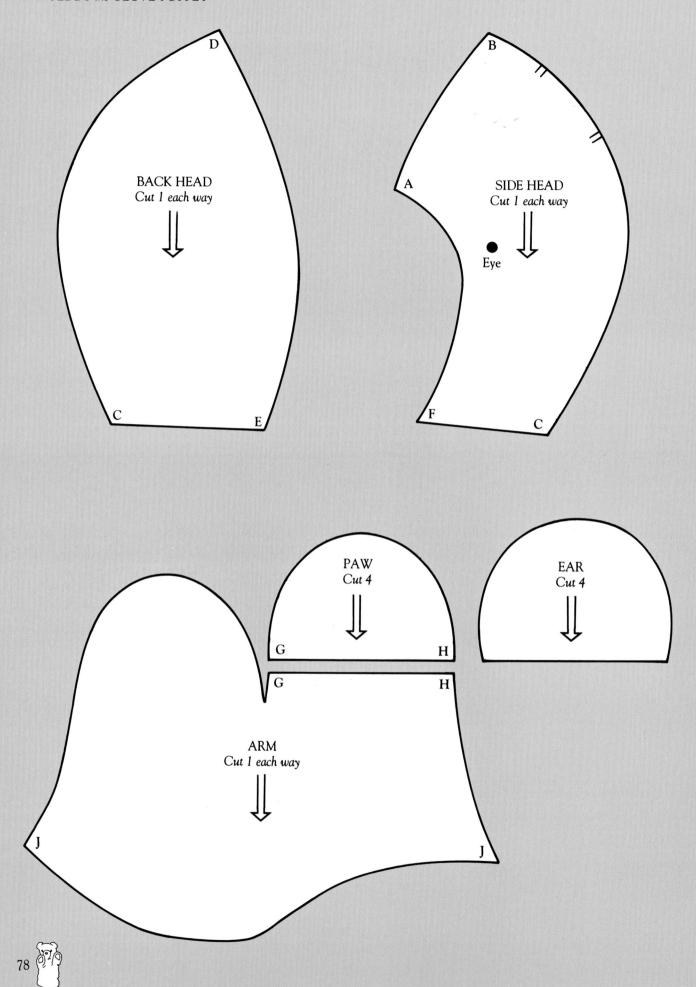

D

BACK HEAD
Cut 1 each way
⇓

C　　　　　　　E

B

A

SIDE HEAD
Cut 1 each way
⇓

● Eye

F　　　　　C

PAW
Cut 4
⇓

G　　　　　H

EAR
Cut 4
⇓

G　　　　　H

ARM
Cut 1 each way
⇓

J　　　　　　　J

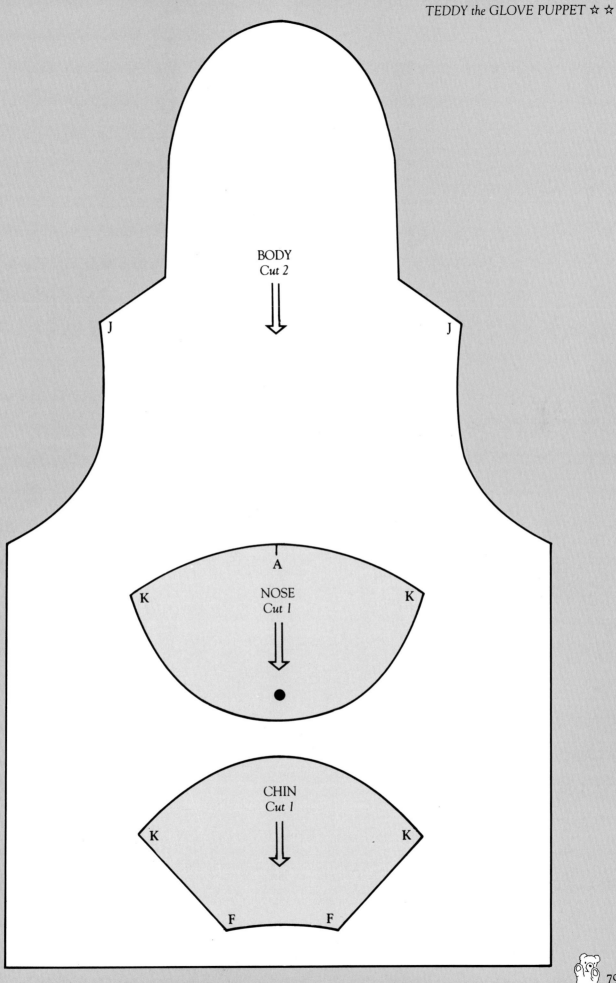

BODY
Cut 2

J

J

A

K

NOSE
Cut 1

K

●

CHIN
Cut 1

K

K

F

F

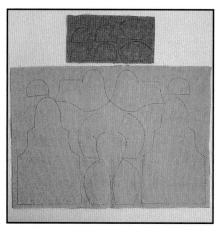

1 Make a pattern (see p.5) and draw around it on the wrong side of the fabric as shown.

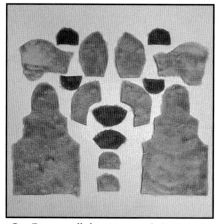

2 Cut out all the pieces and check with the picture that all the sections are there.

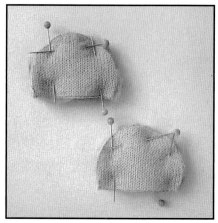

3 With right sides facing, pin the ear pieces together.

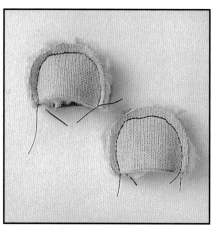

4 Stitch the ear pieces together leaving the straight edges open, as shown.

5 Turn each ear right side out and brush the seams.

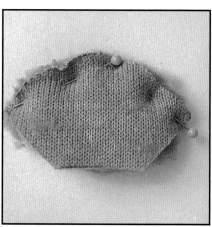

6 With right sides facing, pin nose to chin from **K** to **K**.

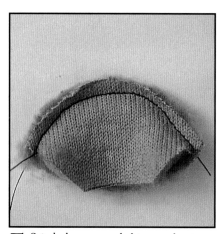

7 Stitch the nose and chin together along the seam line, as shown.

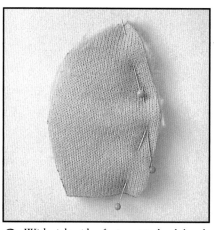

8 With right sides facing, pin back head pieces together from **D** to **E**.

9 Stitch back head pieces together along the seam line, as shown.

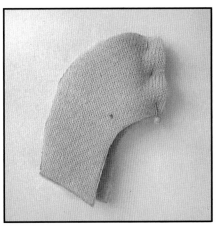

10 *With right sides facing, pin side head pieces together from* **A** *to* **B**.

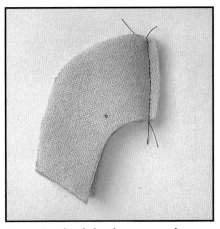

11 *Stitch side head pieces together along the seam line, as shown.*

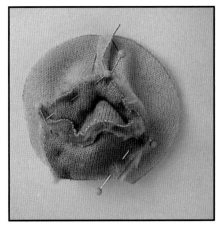

12 *With right sides facing, pin the joined nose and chin to the side head from* **F** *to* **F**.

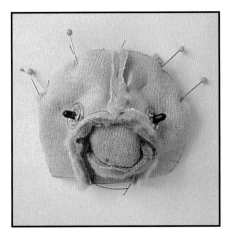

13 *Stitch nose and chin to side head. Insert the eyes (see p.8). With right sides facing, pin ears to face in the positions marked on the template.*

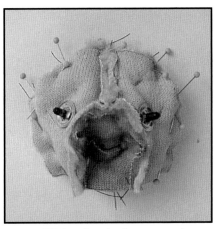

14 *With right sides facing, pin the back head to the face from* **C** *to* **C**.

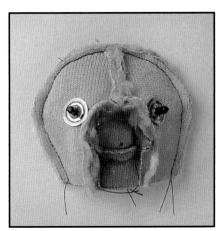

15 *Stitch the back head to face from* **C** *to* **C**, *leaving the bottom edge open.*

16 *Turn head right side out and check that the ears are secure. Brush all seams.*

17 *Stuff the front of the head with filling to achieve a round, full face.*

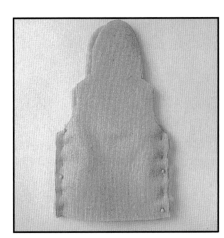

18 *With right sides facing, pin body pieces together along each straight side.*

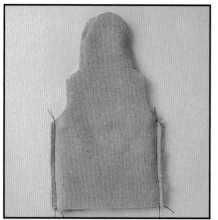

19 Stitch the body pieces together down each side, as shown.

20 Turn up the bottom edge and stitch into place with a zigzag stitch.

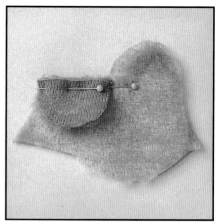

21 With right sides facing, pin a paw to an arm from **H** to **G**.

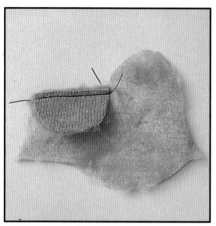

22 Stitch the paw to the arm from **G** to **H**. Repeat steps *21-22* for second paw and arm.

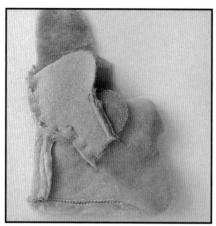

23 Fold top half of body downwards. With right sides facing, pin arm to body matching **J** to **J**.

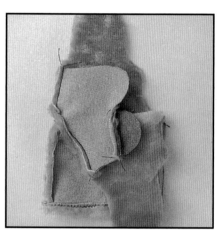

24 Stitch arm to body from **J** to **J**. Repeat steps *23-24* for second arm.

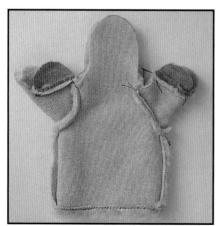

25 Fold body together and arms in half, as shown.

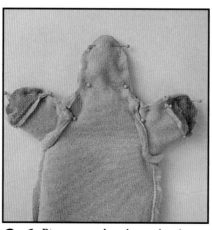

26 Pin arms and neck together from **G** to **G**, as shown.

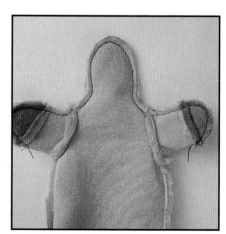

27 Carefully stitch the arms and neck together along the seam line, as shown.

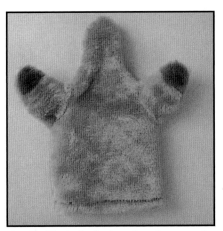

28 *Turn the body right side out and brush all seams.*

29 *Insert neck into head, ensuring that the filling is kept to the front of the face. Position as required.*

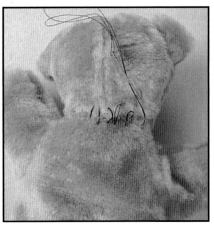

30 *Keeping neck well into the head, stitch together along the neck edge with ladder stitch (see page 8) and secure. Brush the seam.*

TEDDY SHOULDER BAG ☆☆

MATERIALS

- ○ Plush Fur 305mm × 355mm (12″ × 14″)
- ○ Lining 355mm × 255mm (14″ × 10″)
- ○ Zip 205mm (8″)
- ○ Cord 90cm (1yd)
- ○ 2 Small Teddy Eyes
- ○ 1 Medium Teddy Nose

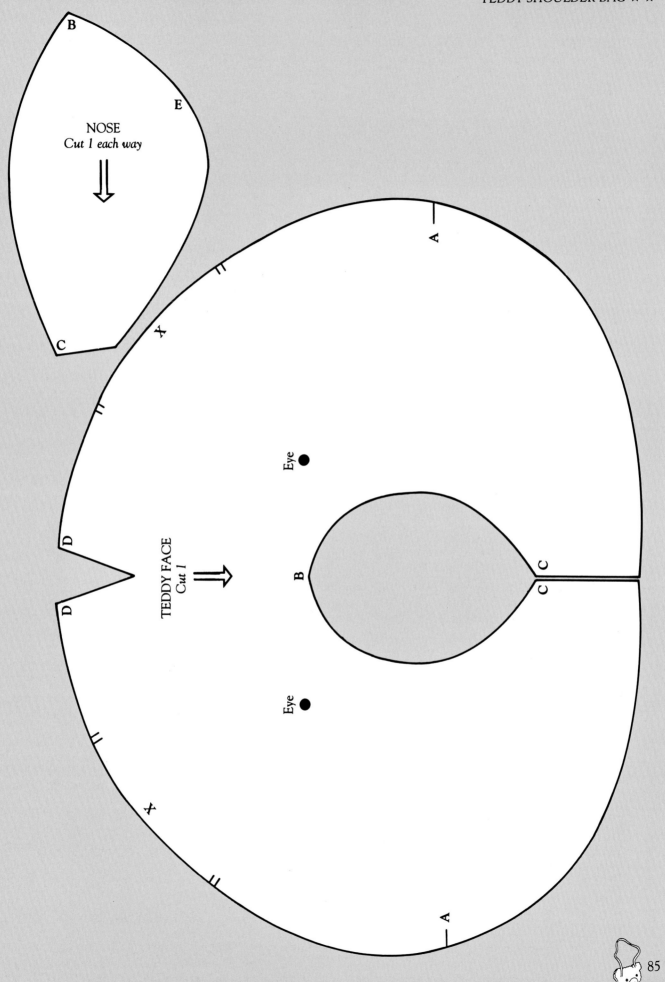

NOSE
Cut 1 each way

⇓

TEDDY FACE
Cut 1 ⇒

Eye ●

Eye ●

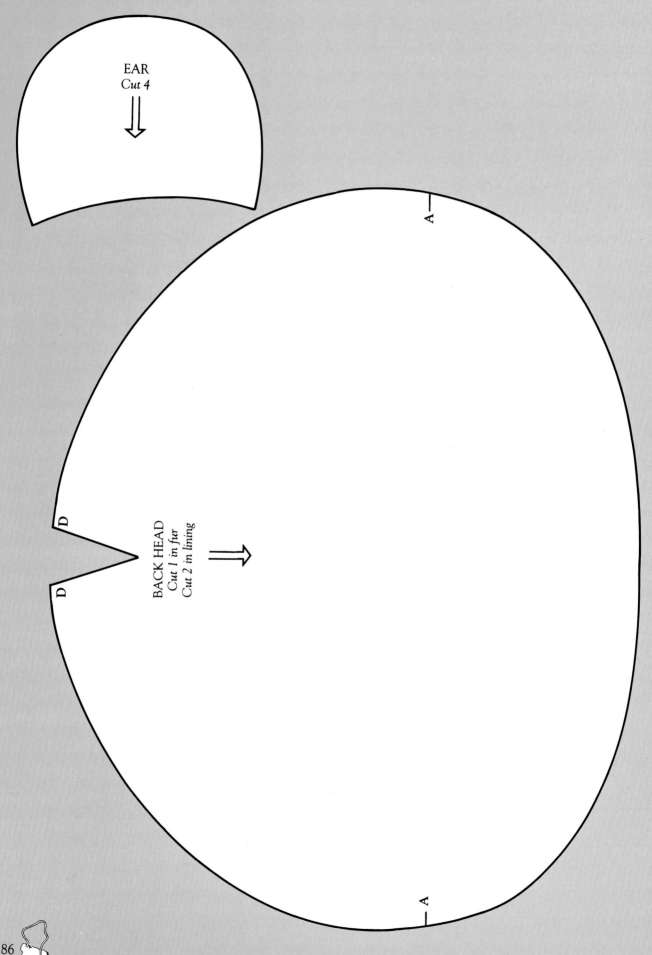

EAR
Cut 4

BACK HEAD
Cut 1 in fur
Cut 2 in lining

D

D

A

A

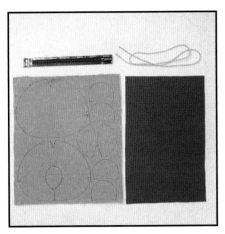

1 Make a pattern (see p.5) and draw around the pieces on the wrong side of the fur fabric and lining. Items required: Zip fastener, Cord.

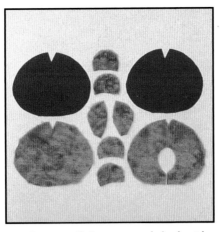

2 Cut out all the pieces and check with the picture that all the sections are there.

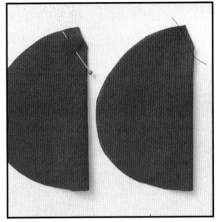

3 With right sides facing, pin and stitch the darts from **D** to **D** on the back head fur and lining pieces.

4 With right sides facing, pin the lining to the back head fur fabric along the bottom edge from **A** to **A**.

5 Stitch the lining to the back head. Snip the seam allowance at **A**.

6 Turn right side out and tack from **A** all around to **A**, as shown.

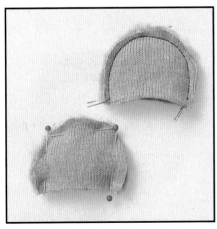

7 With right sides facing, pin and stitch the ear pieces together, leaving the straight edges open.

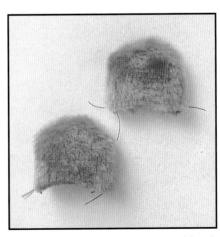

8 Turn the ears right side out and brush the seams.

9 With right sides facing, pin and stitch the nose pieces together from **B** to **E**.

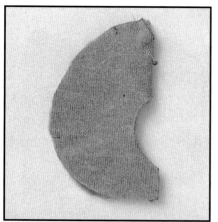

10 With right sides facing, fold the face in half and pin and stitch the dart from **D** to **D**.

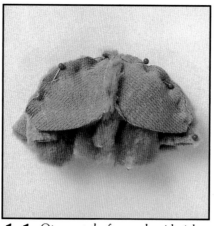

11 Open out the face and, with right sides facing, pin the nose to the face, matching **B** to **C** and **C** to **B**.

12 Stitch the nose to the face along the seam line.

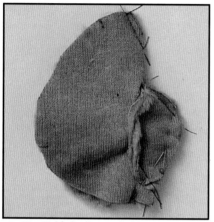

13 Fold the face in half once again, right sides facing, and pin from **E** to neck edge.

14 Stitch the remaining part of the nose along the seam line and brush the seam.

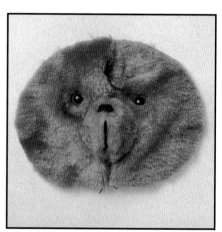

15 Insert the eyes and nose and embroider the bear's mouth (see p.8).

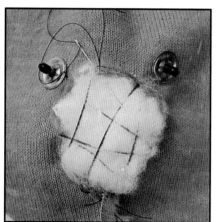

16 Stuff the nose firmly with the filling. To keep the filling in place, sew with a long thread from side to side of the nose, catching in the seam allowance.

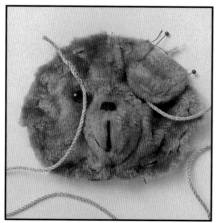

17 Secure the lining to the face. Pin the ends of the cord to the face at mark **X**. Pin ears in place, over cord, as shown.

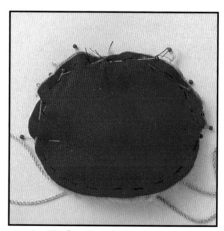

18 With right sides facing, pin the face to the back head, matching **A** to **A**. Check that the ears are secured in the stitching line.

19 Stitch from **A** to **A** and neaten seams with a zigzag stitch.

20 Turn right side out and brush the seams. Insert the zip into the opening and stitch in by hand.

21 Picture shows the completed shoulder bag with the zip hand-sewn into place.

MUMMY and DADDY MOUSE ☆☆☆

MATERIALS
DADDY MOUSE

○ Grey Polished Fur 275mm (11″) × 250mm (10″).

○ White Polished Fur 180mm (7″) × 75mm (3″).

○ Pink Felt for Nightcap 250mm (10″) × 180mm (7″).

○ Striped Material 385mm (15″) × 300mm (12″).

○ White Lining 385mm (15″) × 300mm (12″).

○ Small piece Black Felt.

○ Small piece Yellow Felt.

○ 1 White Bobble.

○ 2 Small Black Eyes.

○ ½ metre Ribbon.

MATERIALS
MUMMY MOUSE

○ Grey Polished Fur 275mm (11″) × 250mm (10″).

○ Pink Polished Fur 180mm (7″) × 75mm (3″).

○ Patterned Material 385mm (15″) × 275mm (11″).

○ White Lining 385mm (15″) × 275mm (11″).

○ Thin Cotton for Bonnet 300mm (12″) × 100mm (4″).

○ Lace 1 metre × 12mm (½″)

○ Pink Felt 125mm (5″) × 75mm (3″).

○ 2 Small Black Eyes.

○ 1 White Bobble.

○ ½ metre Ribbon.

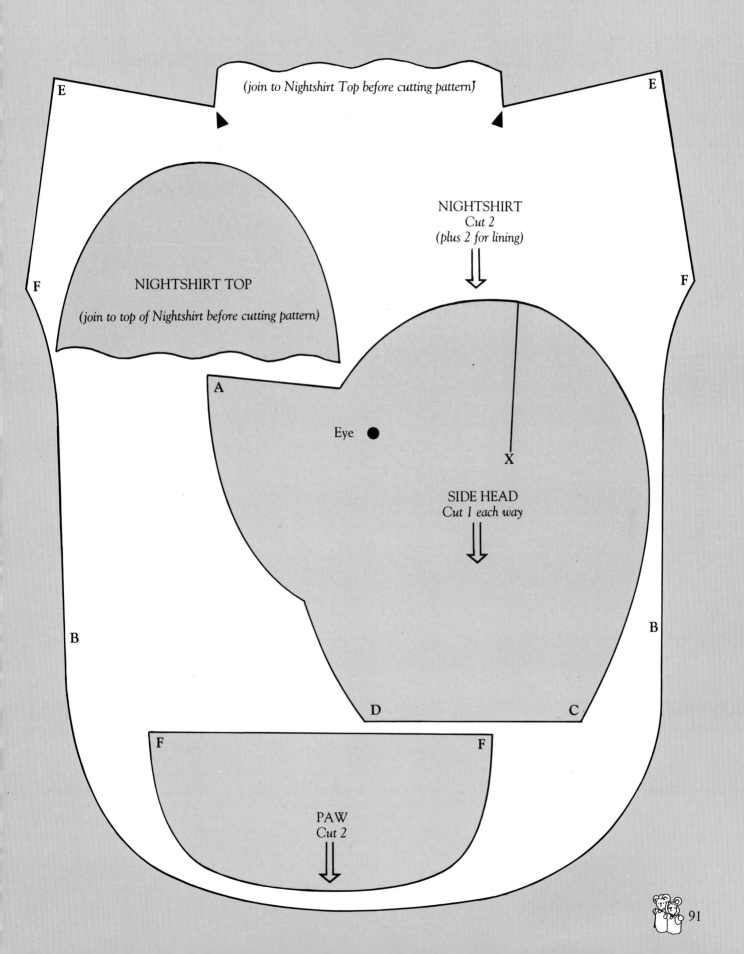

E

E

(join to Nightshirt Top before cutting pattern)

NIGHTSHIRT
Cut 2
(plus 2 for lining)

F

F

NIGHTSHIRT TOP

(join to top of Nightshirt before cutting pattern)

A

Eye ●

X

SIDE HEAD
Cut 1 each way

B

B

D

C

F

F

PAW
Cut 2

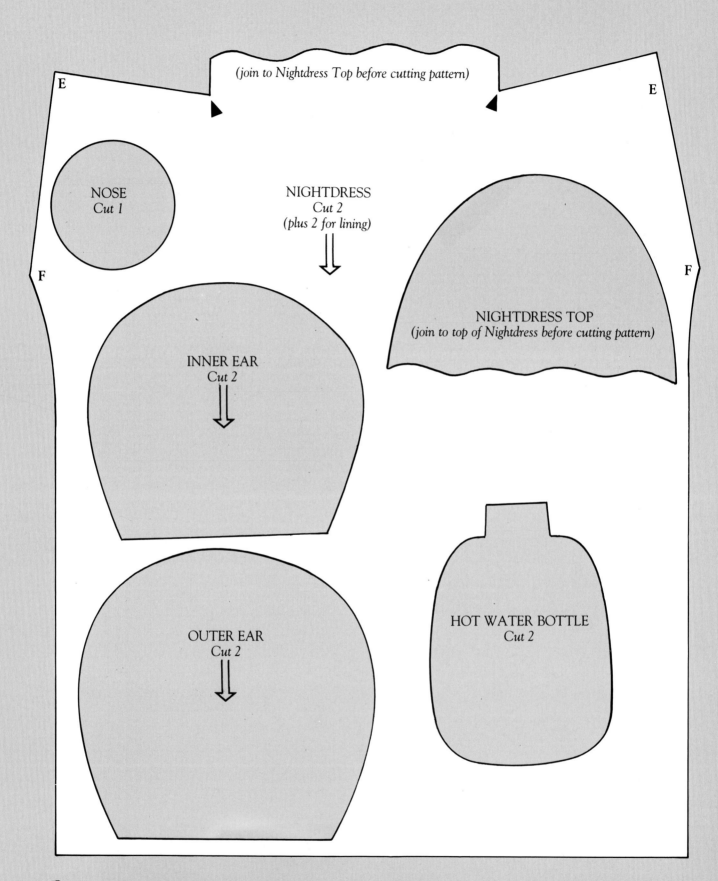

NOSE
Cut 1

NIGHTDRESS
Cut 2
(plus 2 for lining)

(join to Nightdress Top before cutting pattern)

E   E

F   F

NIGHTDRESS TOP
(join to top of Nightdress before cutting pattern)

INNER EAR
Cut 2

OUTER EAR
Cut 2

HOT WATER BOTTLE
Cut 2

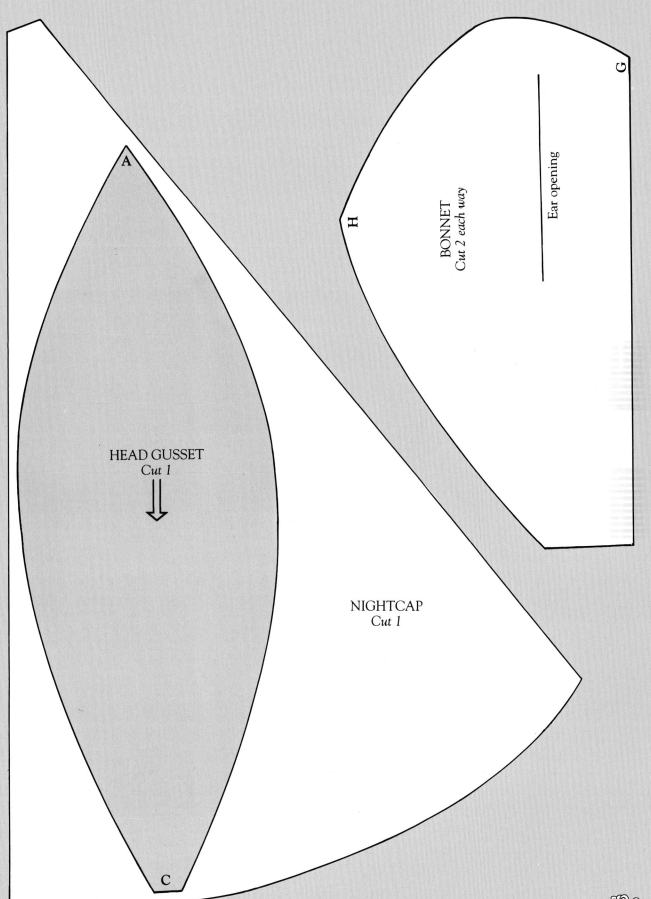

A

HEAD GUSSET
Cut 1

⇓

C

H

BONNET
Cut 2 each way

Ear opening

G

NIGHTCAP
Cut 1

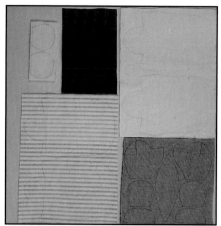

1 Make a pattern of each template shape required (see p.5) for Daddy Mouse. Then draw around each pattern on the wrong side of the appropriate material, as shown.

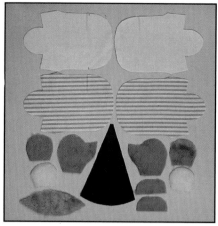

2 Cut out all pieces and then check with the picture that all the sections are there.

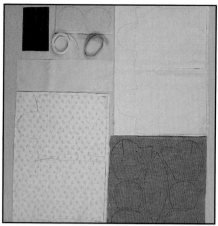

3 Make a pattern of each template shape required (see p.5) for Mummy Mouse. Then draw around each pattern on the wrong side of the appropriate material, as shown.

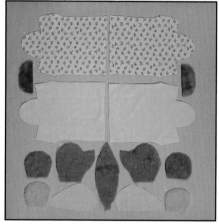

4 Cut out all pieces and then check with the picture that all the sections are there.

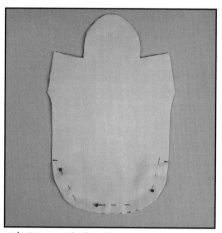

5 Pin a nightshirt lining to a nightshirt fabric, right sides facing. Pin from **B** to **B**, along the bottom edge.

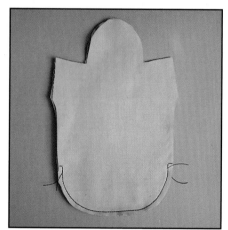

6 Stitch along the bottom edge of the nightshirt as shown.

7 Carefully snip at **B** to seam line on each side of the nightshirt. Repeat steps 4-7 for second side. Turn each piece right side out.

8 Tack material matching the edges. Repeat steps 5-8 for second side.

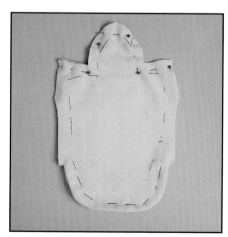

9 Pin top edge together from **E** to **E**, right sides facing.

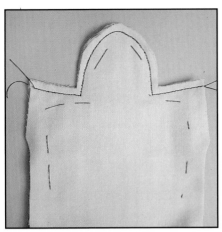

10 Stitch along the top edge from **E** to **E** joining the two sides together.

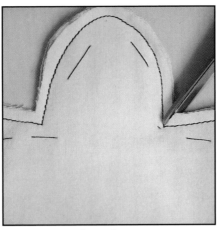

11 Snip at the neck corners to ease the seams. Unfold the nightshirt to the right side and lay flat.

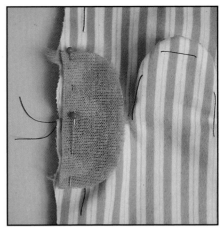

12 Pin a paw to each side matching mark **F** to **F**, right sides facing.

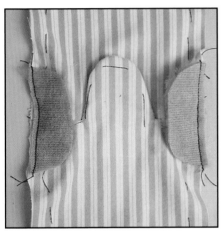

13 Stitch each paw to nightshirt, tapering off each side as shown.

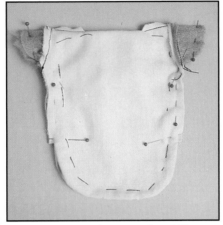

14 Open out the paws, then fold nightshirt in half, right sides facing. Pin each side together from centre paw to position mark **B**.

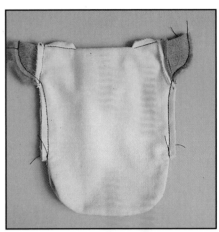

15 Stitch from top to **B**, on each side of the nightshirt. Carefully remove the tacking stitches.

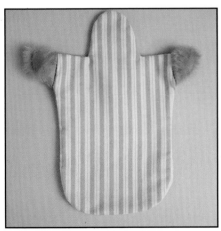

16 Turn right side out and check that all seams are correctly stitched. Brush the fur paws then press nightshirt with a cool iron.

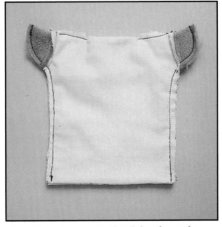

17 Repeat steps 5-15 for the nightdress of Mummy Mouse.

18 Turn right side out. Press material. Stitch lace along bottom edge. Brush the fur paws.

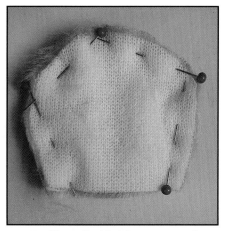

19 Using Daddy Mouse materials, pin each inner ear to each outer ear right sides facing, as shown.

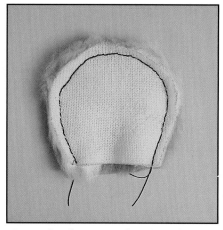

20 Stitch ears together along the outer edge, leaving bottom open.

21 Turn each ear right side out and brush all seams.

22 Starting at mark **A** pin side head to head gusset finishing at mark **C**.

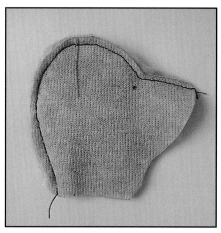

23 Carefully stitch side head to head gusset as shown. Turn head over with gusset uppermost.

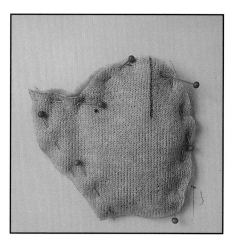

24 Pin second side head to gusset, from mark **D** to mark **C**.

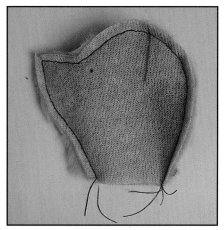

25 Carefully stitch the pieces together leaving the bottom open, as shown.

26 Starting at **X** on side head, carefully cut ear opening across top of head gusset and down to **X** on second side.

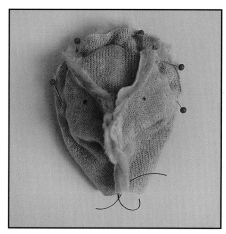

27 Insert ears (with inner ears facing towards nose), into ear opening and pin into position. Then pin seam from **X** to **X**.

28 Stitch ear opening seams, tapering off as shown.

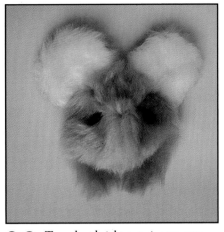

29 Turn head right out, insert eyes (see p. 8), then brush all seams.

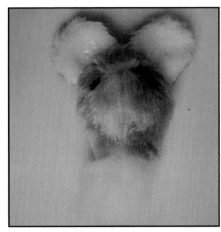

30 Stuff the front half of the head to fill-out the face.

31 Insert hand into nightshirt and place head over the top piece, keeping the stuffing forward.

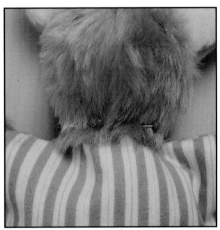

32 Align head with body and pin in position around the neck, using seam allowance as shown.

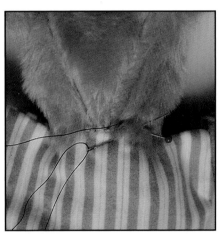

33 Keeping hand in puppet, stitch carefully and firmly around the neck with ladder stitch. Secure thread.

34 With strong thread, sew running stitch around edge of felt for nose.

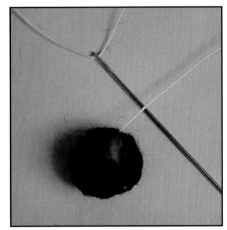

35 Place small amount of stuffing in centre, pull up thread and fasten. Roll between hands to make round nose shape.

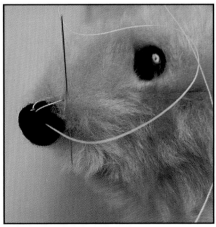

36 Stitch nose firmly into place with ladder stitch as shown.

37 *Picture shows Daddy Mouse so far.*

38 *Repeat steps 19-36 using the materials for Mummy Mouse.*

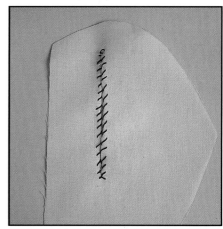

39 *Cut ear opening in bonnet. Oversew the cut edges to neaten, as shown. Repeat for second side.*

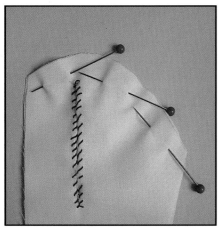

40 *Place both sides together and pin from **H** to **G**.*

41 *Stitch from **G** to **H**, open out. Then stitch lace around outer edge.*

42 *Stitch ribbon to short side and flowers near top of ear opening, as shown. Tie onto Mummy Mouse's head.*

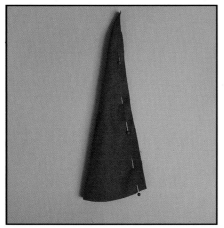

43 *Fold nightcap in half and pin along edge.*

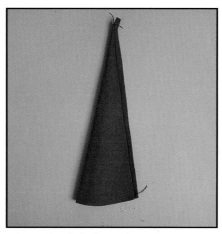

44 *Stitch the long edge together to form the nightcap shape.*

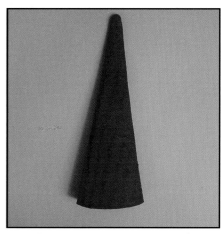

45 *Turn right side out and pull into shape.*

46 *Stitch a bobble to top. Lightly stuff and then sew onto Daddy Mouse's head. Tie ribbon around neck.*

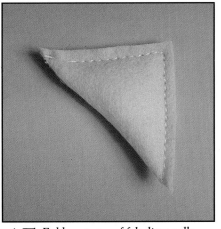

47 *Fold a square of felt diagonally, insert small amount of stuffing and stitch along edges to make a cheese, as shown. Sew to Daddy Mouse's paw.*

48 *Pin hot water bottle sides together with small amount of filling in centre. Stitch around edge and then sew it to Mummy Mouse's paw.*

JACK the RABBIT ☆☆☆

MATERIALS

○ White Fur 475mm (19″) × 350mm (14″).

○ Pink Fur 125mm (5″) × 125mm (5″).

○ Orange Felt 90mm (3½″) × 100mm (4″).

○ Green Felt 20mm (1″) × 20mm (1″).

○ 2 Medium Goo Goo Eyes.

○ 1 Black Nose.

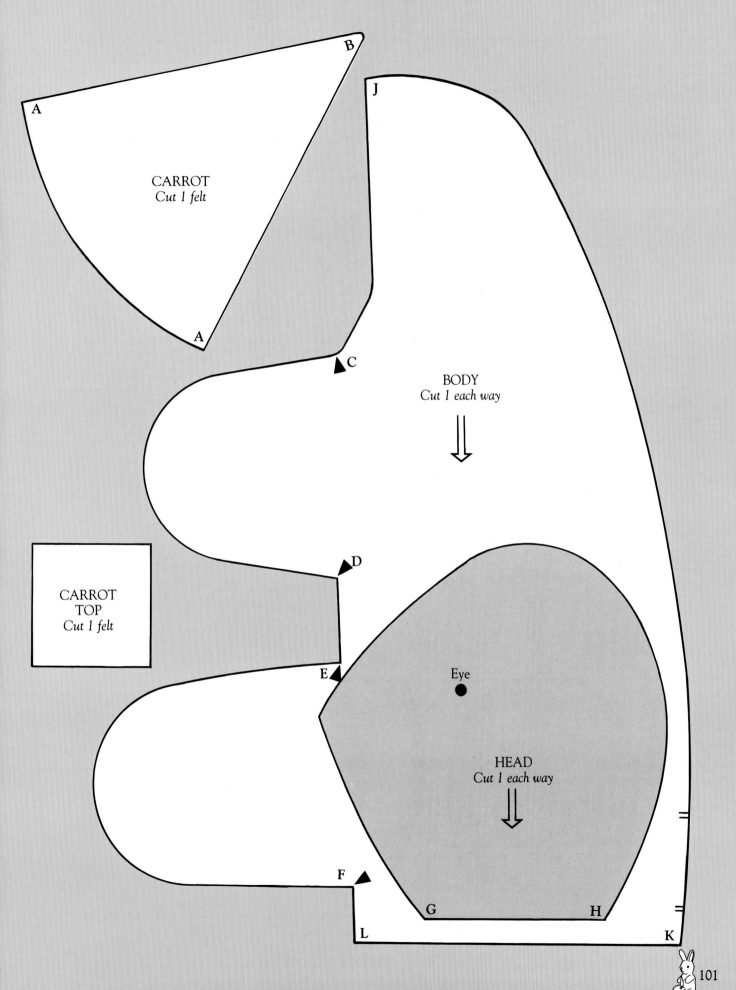

CARROT
Cut 1 felt

A

B

A

J

C

BODY
Cut 1 each way

D

CARROT
TOP
Cut 1 felt

E

Eye

HEAD
Cut 1 each way

F

G

H

L

K

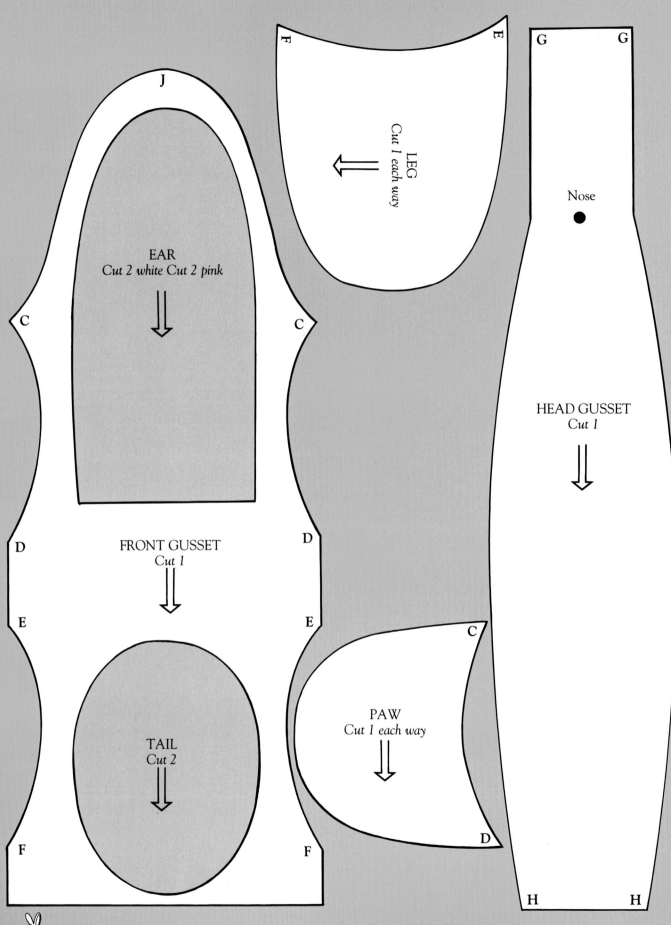

J

EAR
Cut 2 white Cut 2 pink

C

C

D

FRONT GUSSET
Cut 1

D

E

E

F

TAIL
Cut 2

F

F

LEG
Cut 1 each way

E

C

D

PAW
Cut 1 each way

G

G

Nose

HEAD GUSSET
Cut 1

H

H

1 Make a pattern of each template shape required (see p.5). Then draw around each pattern on the wrong side of the appropriate material, as shown.

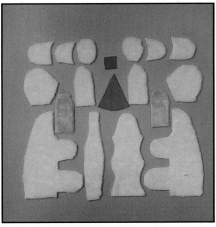

2 Cut out all pieces and then check with the picture that all the sections are there.

3 Pin inner ear to outer ear, right sides facing. Repeat for second ear.

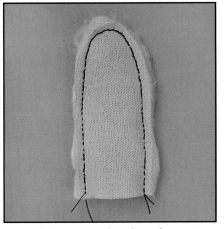

4 Stitch ears together along the outer edge, leaving bottom open.

5 Turn each ear right side out and brush seams. Fold and pin ears as shown.

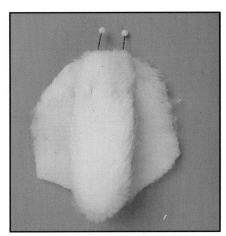

6 Position an ear on each side head as shown. Pin in place.

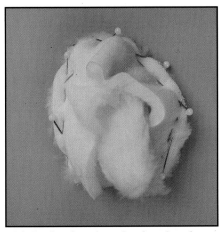

7 Pin head gusset to head, right sides together, matching at **G** and finishing at **H**.

8 Carefully stitch head from **H** to **G**.

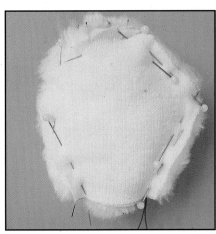

9 Place second head to gusset, right sides facing, and pin from **H** to **G**.

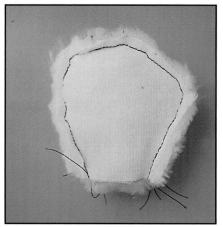

10 *Carefully stitch around head, leaving the neck open. Insert eyes (see p. 8).*

11 *Turn head right side out and brush all seams. Insert nose (see p.8).*

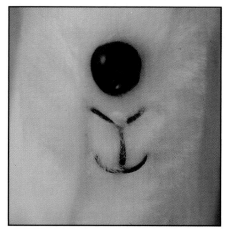

12 *Embroider bunny mouth with stranded cotton (see p.8). Stuff front of head.*

13 *Pin a leg to the front gusset, matching* **F** *and* **E***, then a paw at* **C** *and* **D***. Repeat for remaining leg and paw.*

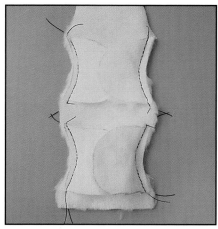

14 *Stitch legs and paws into place as shown following the stitching line. Unfold and brush all seams.*

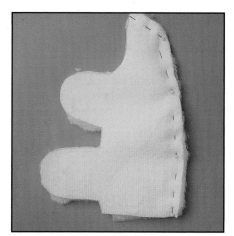

15 *Place body pieces together, right sides facing, and pin from* **J** *to* **K***.*

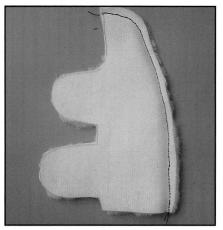

16 *Stitch body together. Unfold and brush seam.*

17 *Place front on back, right sides facing, and pin all round from* **L** *to* **L** *matching all marked positions.*

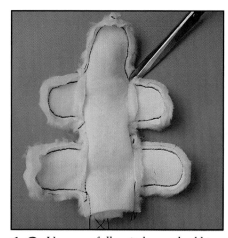

18 *Very carefully stitch round rabbit from* **L** *to* **L** *leaving base open. Cut all ease points.*

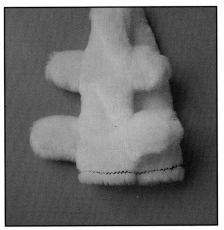

19 *Carefully turn right side out and brush all seams. Using seam allowance, neaten opening with zigzag stitch.*

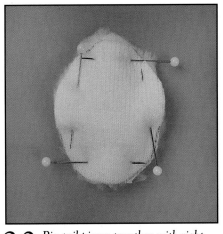

20 *Pin tail pieces together with right sides facing.*

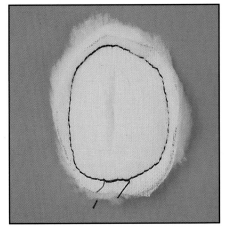

21 *Stitch all round edge of tail. Cut a small opening in one side as shown.*

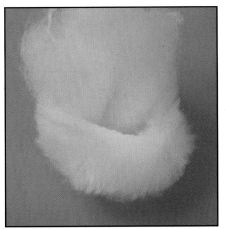

22 *Turn tail right side out and brush seams. Stuff with a small amount of filling.*

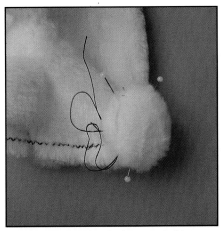

23 *Stitch tail to body using ladder stitch and secure the thread.*

24 *Place hand in puppet, slide head over top of body positioning as required.*

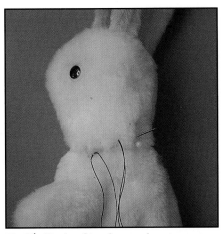

25 *Pin head in place and, using seam allowance, sew head to body firmly.*

26 *Fold carrot in half, pin and stitch along the edge.*

27 *Turn right side out and pull into carrot shape.*

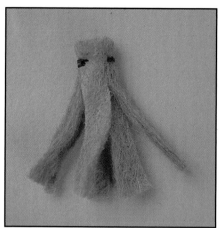

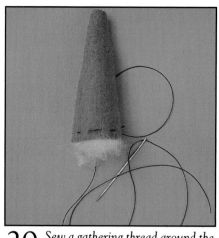

28 *Roll up square of felt for carrot top and stitch one end. Cut to form fringe for the carrot top.*

29 *Sew a gathering thread around the base of the carrot. Stuff lightly, pull up thread and secure.*

30 *Stitch carrot top to the carrot. Shape carrot with a few stitches as shown. Stitch carrot to Jack's paw.*

PATRICK the FOX ☆☆☆

MATERIALS

- Tan Long Fur 510mm (20″) × 385mm (15″).
- Cream Polished Fur 125mm (5″) × 75mm (3″).
- White Polished Fur 150mm (6″) × 100mm (4″).
- 2 Medium Teddy Eyes.
- 1 Animal Nose.

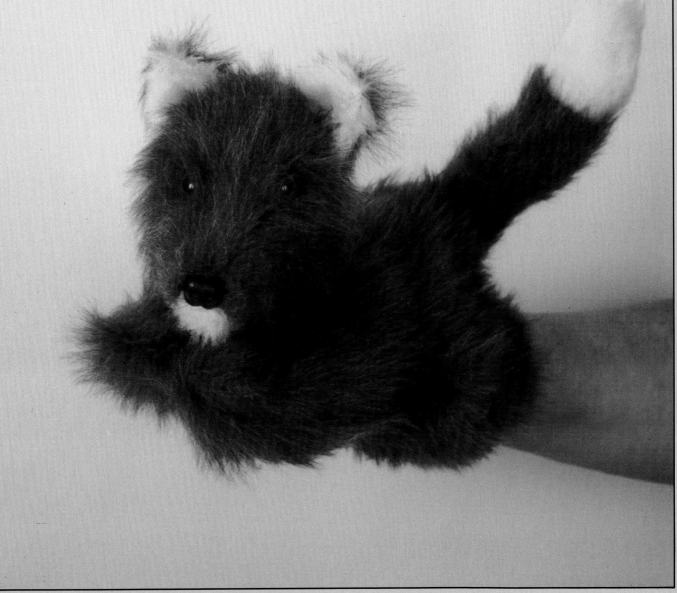

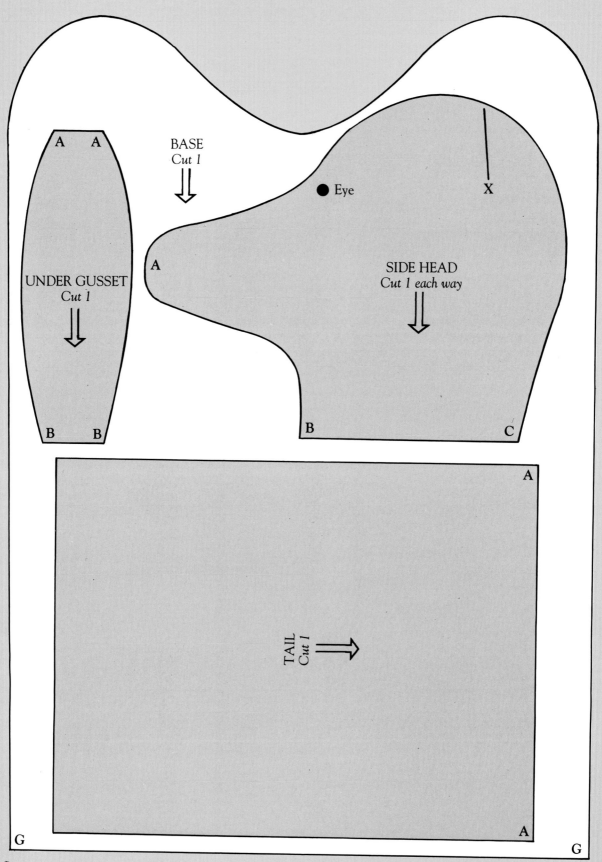

A A

BASE
Cut 1
⬇

● Eye

X

A

UNDER GUSSET
Cut 1
⬇

SIDE HEAD
Cut 1 each way
⬇

B B

B

C

A

TAIL
Cut 1
➡

G

A

G

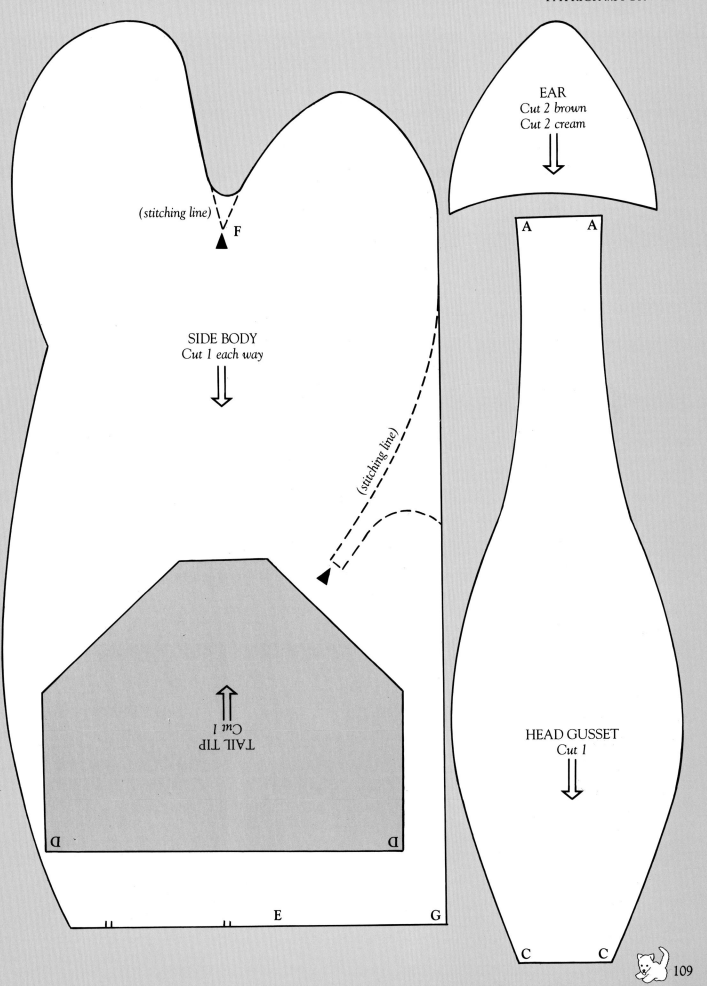

EAR
Cut 2 brown
Cut 2 cream

(stitching line)

▲ F

SIDE BODY
Cut 1 each way

(stitching line)

▲

TAIL TIP
Cut 1

D   D

E   G

A   A

HEAD GUSSET
Cut 1

C   C

1 *Make a pattern of each template shape required (see p.5). Then draw around each pattern on the wrong side of the appropriate material, as shown.*

2 *Cut out all pieces and then check with the picture that all the sections are there.*

3 *Pin tail tip to tail, right sides facing, matching at* **D**.

4 *Stitch together and then unfold as shown. Brush seam.*

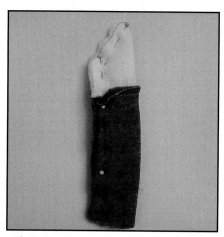

5 *Fold tail in half lengthways, then pin top and side edge together leaving bottom open.*

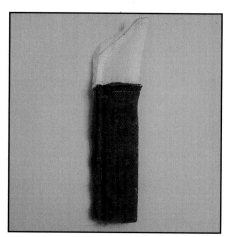

6 *Stitch the tail leaving bottom open.*

7 *Turn tail right side out and brush the seams.*

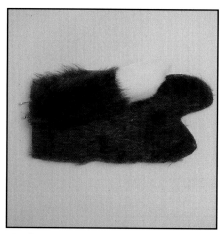

8 *Pin in position to side body.*

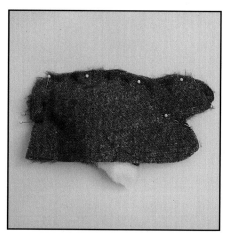

9 *Pin second side body to first from mark* **E** *to mark* **F**, *right sides facing.*

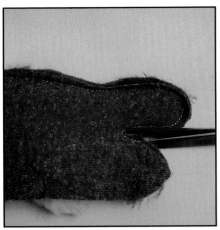

10 *Stitch from mark **E** to mark **F**, then snip to seam line at **F**.*

11 *Open the body and place onto the base, right sides facing. Pin along the right side of the body from **G** to paw, following the stitching line.*

12 *Stitch together following the stitching line, from paw to **G**.*

13 *Open out body, turn up seam allowance and sew along bottom edge with zigzag stitch.*

14 *Refold the body, right sides facing and pin along the left side, following the stitching line.*

15 *Stitch from **G**, then under neck to paw. Snip at ease points, as shown.*

16 *Carefully turn right side out and brush all seams.*

17 *Pin each brown ear to each cream ear, right sides facing.*

18 *Stitch each ear together, leaving the bottom edges open.*

19 Turn each ear right side out and brush seams.

20 Pin head gusset to under gusset at mark **A**, as shown.

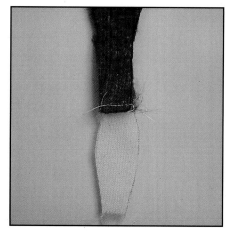

21 Stitch the two gussets together and then unfold.

22 Pin side head to gusset, from **C**, to **A** then to **B**, right sides facing. Then stitch together.

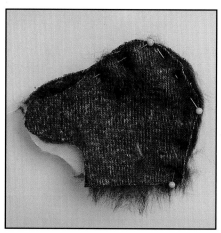

23 Pin and stitch second side head to gusset, right sides facing, from **B** to **C**. Leave the bottom edge open.

24 Starting at mark **X** on side head, carefully cut ear opening across top of head gusset and down to mark **X** on second side head.

25 Insert ears into ear opening and pin from **X** to **X**.

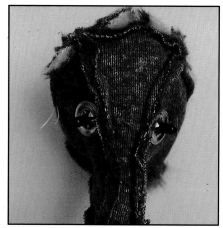

26 Stitch into place, tapering off ends. Insert safety eyes (see p.8).

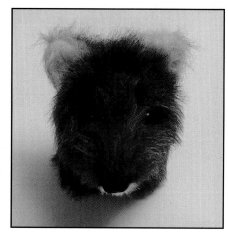

27 Gently turn head right side out and insert the nose. Brush all seams.

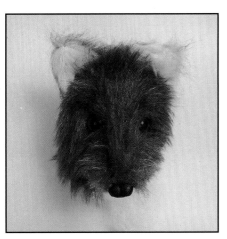

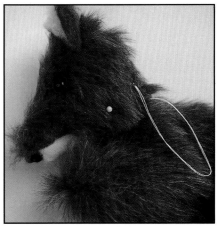

28 *Stuff the front of the head firmly to fill-out the face. Keep back of head free for fingers.*

29 *Place hand inside body and position head over neck, keeping the filling to the front.*

30 *Turn up seam allowance on head, pin and stitch into place. Brush all seams.*

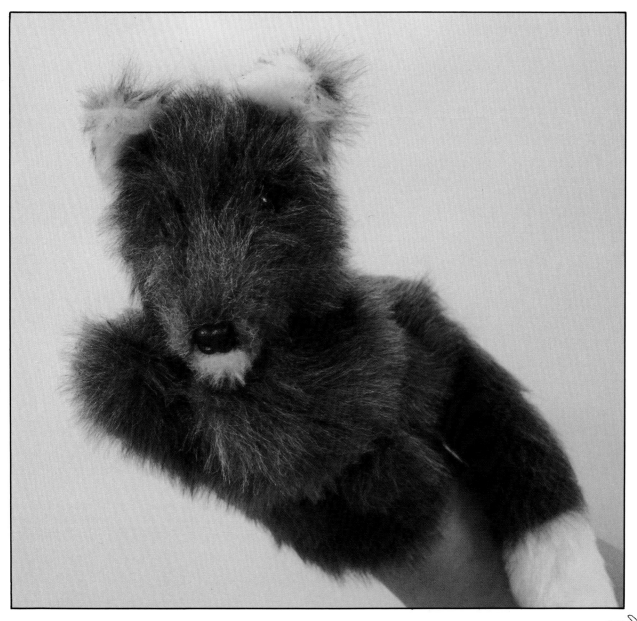

PERKY the PUPPY ☆☆☆

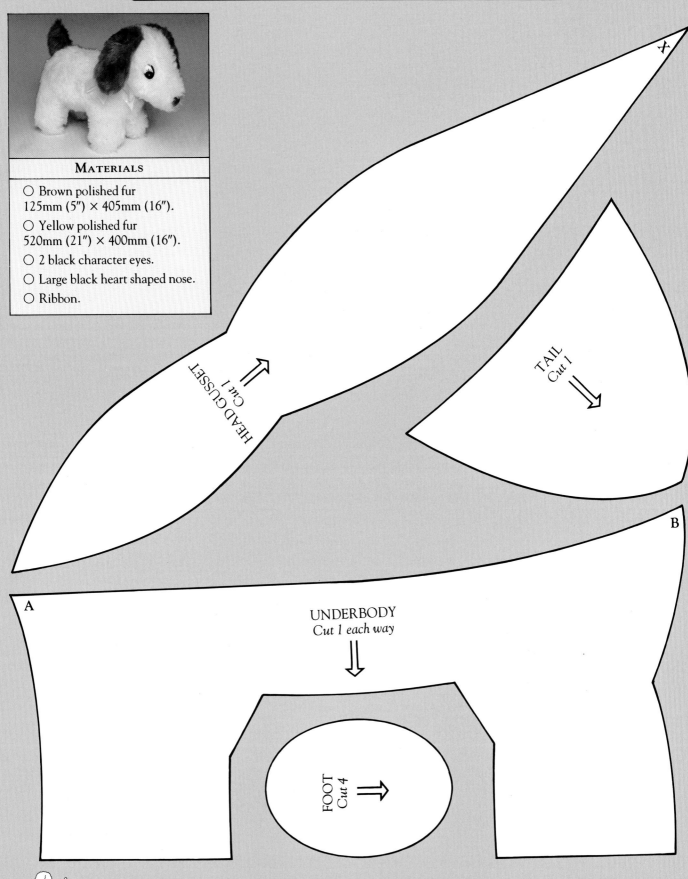

MATERIALS

○ Brown polished fur
125mm (5") × 405mm (16").

○ Yellow polished fur
520mm (21") × 400mm (16").

○ 2 black character eyes.

○ Large black heart shaped nose.

○ Ribbon.

X

HEAD GUSSET
Cut 1

TAIL
Cut 1

A

B

UNDERBODY
Cut 1 each way

FOOT
Cut 4

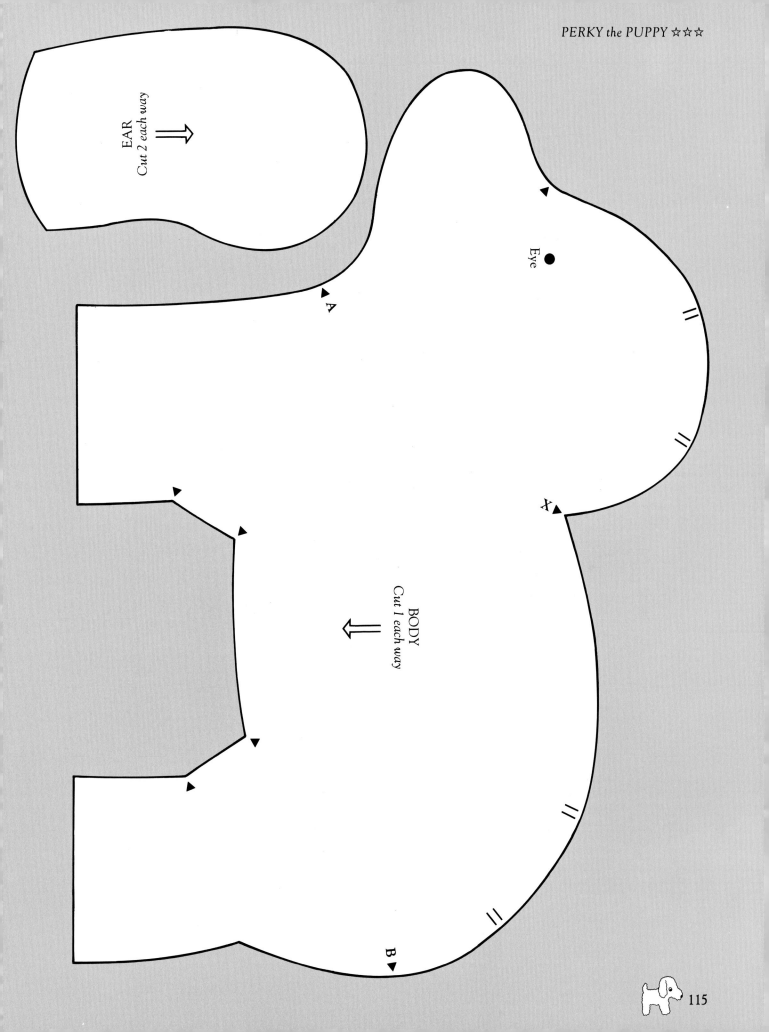

EAR
Cut 2 each way
⟹

A ►

● Eye

=

X ►

BODY
Cut 1 each way
⟸

=

=

B ►

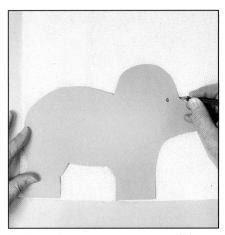

1 To make a pattern, trace round the templates and transfer to thin card.

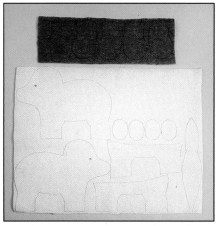

2 Place pattern on wrong side of fabric and draw around all pieces.

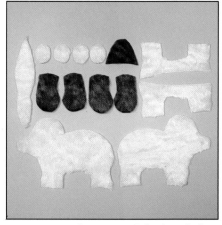

3 Cut out all pieces and check with the picture that all the sections are there.

4 Pin a pair of ears with right sides together.

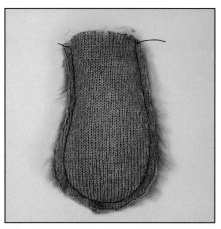

5 Stitch the two pieces together leaving the top open as shown.

6 Carefully turn the ear through to right side, using the thumb as shown.

7 Using the blunt end of a pencil, ease the inside top end into an even curve.

8 Gently brush fur at seams.

9 Repeat steps *4-8* for the other ear.

10 *Fold tail in half lengthways. Pin and stitch the longest side. Turn through to right side and then brush the seam.*

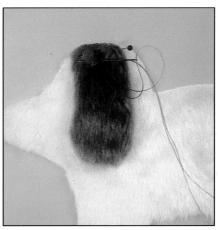

11 *Pin and tack an ear to each body piece in position shown.*

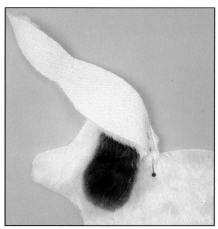

12 *Pin head gusset to back of neck matching at* **X**.

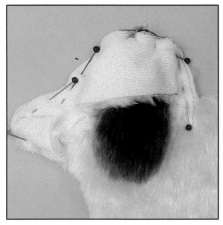

13 *Continue pinning the gusset over the head, round the nose and under the chin.*

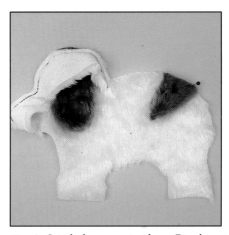

14 *Stitch the gusset in place. Pin the tail in position pointing towards front paw.*

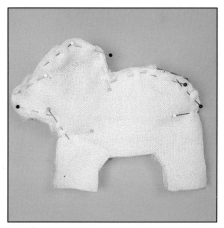

15 *With right sides facing, place second body on first side and, matching at* **A** *and* **B**, *carefully pin in place.*

16 *Stitch from* **A** *to* **B** *as shown.*

17 *Cut carefully at end of stitch line and easing points.*

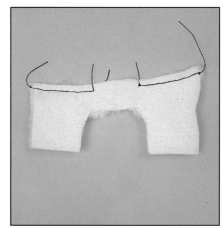

18 *With right sides facing, pin under-bodies together. Stitch along top edge leaving an opening as shown.*

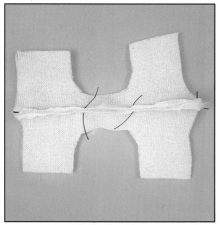

19 *Lay underbodies flat, wrong side upwards.*

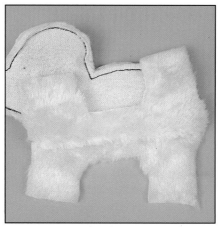

20 *Lift up top side of body as shown. Place underbody on top (matching **A**'s and **B**'s) and pin round, leaving bottom of legs open.*

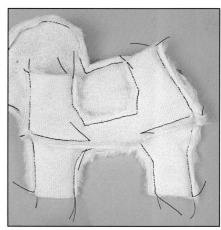

21 *Stitch underbody to body as shown.*

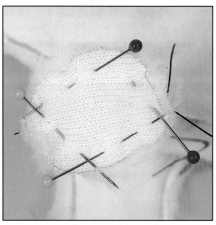

22 *Open bottom of leg and pin on a foot (right sides together).*

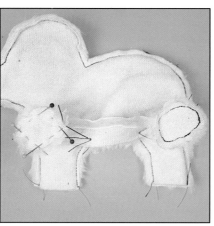

23 *Carefully stitch the foot in place. Repeat for each remaining foot.*

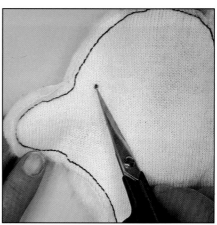

24 *Make a small hole at each marked eye position and insert eye (see p.8).*

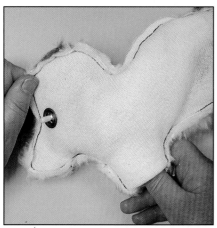

25 *Gently push each leg into body.*

26 *Push head into centre and out through the underbody opening.*

27 *Continue turning right side out, easing seams at curves. Insert nose (see p.8).*

28 *Brush all seams.*

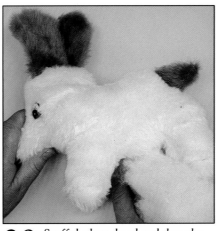

29 *Stuff the legs, head and then the body with sufficient filling to achieve a firm, but not hard, result.*

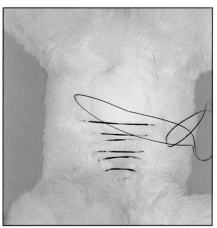

30 *Close the opening with ladder stitch (see p.8). Brush carefully all over. Tie on a ribbon bow.*

JUMBO the ELEPHANT ☆☆☆

MATERIALS

- ○ Blue polished fur 405mm (16″) × 265mm (10½″).
- ○ White polished fur 110mm (4½″) × 88mm (3½″).
- ○ 2 medium goo goo eyes.
- ○ Ribbon.

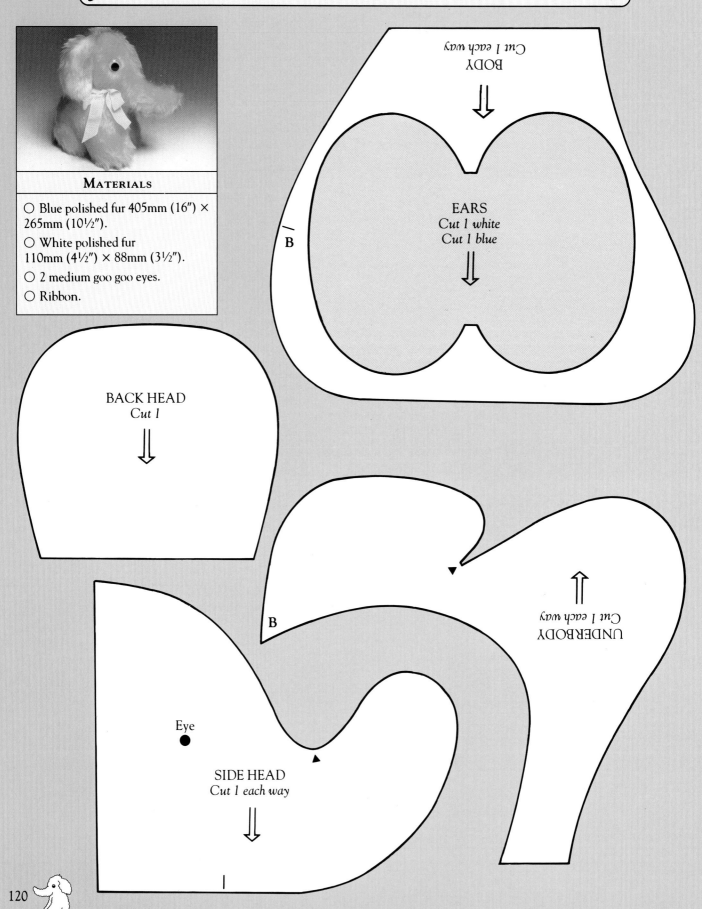

BODY
Cut 1 each way

EARS
Cut 1 white
Cut 1 blue

B

BACK HEAD
Cut 1

UNDERBODY
Cut 1 each way

B

Eye

SIDE HEAD
Cut 1 each way

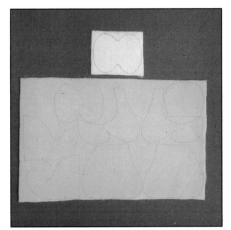

1 Make a pattern (see p.5) and draw around it on the wrong side of the fabric as shown.

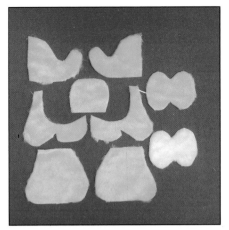

2 Cut out all pieces and check with the picture that all the sections are there.

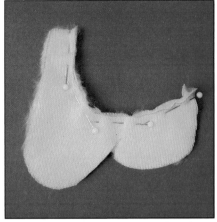

3 Pin together underbodies, right sides facing.

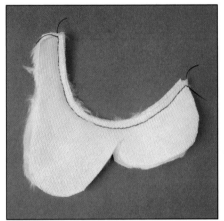

4 Stitch the two pieces together.

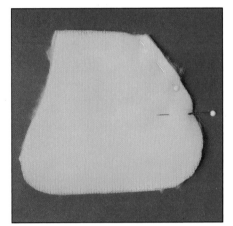

5 Pin body pieces, with right sides together, up to point marked **B**. Stitch.

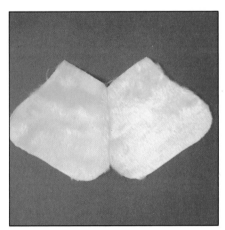

6 Open out body pieces and brush seam.

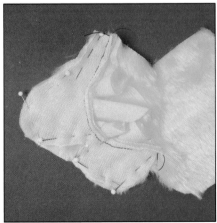

7 Place underbody on to body piece, right sides together, matching at **B**. Pin as shown.

8 Carry on pinning underbody to body until neck is reached. Leave neck open.

9 Carefully stitch all round body. Snip at corners making sure that stitching is not cut.

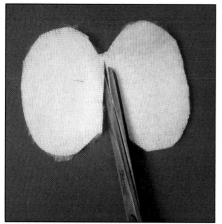

10 Cut ear pieces in half, as shown.

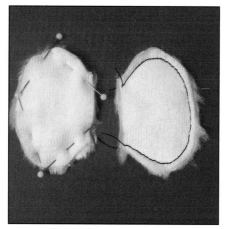

11 Place white ears on top of coloured, right sides facing. Stitch as shown.

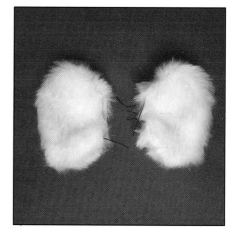

12 Turn ears through to right side, easing edges with blunt end of a pencil. Brush seams.

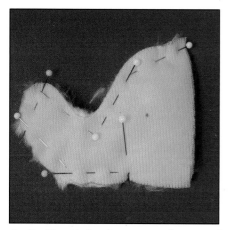

13 Pin side head pieces together up to **A**.

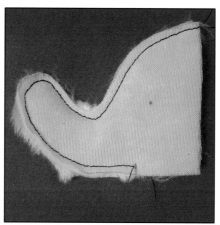

14 Stitch side head pieces together.

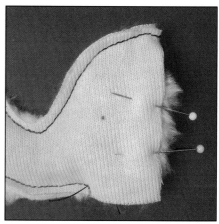

15 Pin ears to edge of head as shown.

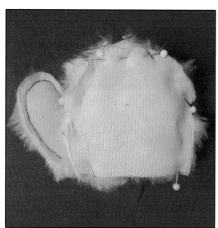

16 Starting at bottom of back-head, pin to side head with right sides together. Continue round the curved sides of the back-head to the bottom of second side.

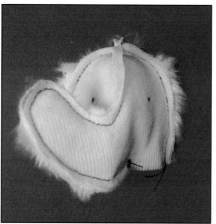

17 Stitch trunk to back head, leaving straight edge open. Insert eyes (see p.8).

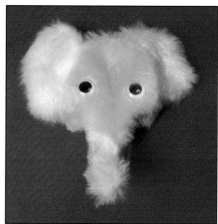

18 Turn inside out. Brush seams.

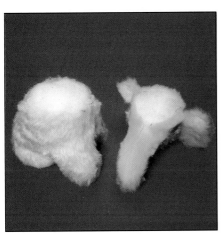

19 *Stuff head and body with sufficient filling to achieve a firm, but not result.*

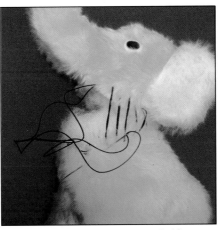

20 *Stitch head to body using ladder stitch (see p.8), matching at centre front and back. Pull thread up tightly and secure.*

21 *Brush all over and tie ribbon around neck with a double knot and bow.*

JENNY the DONKEY ☆☆☆

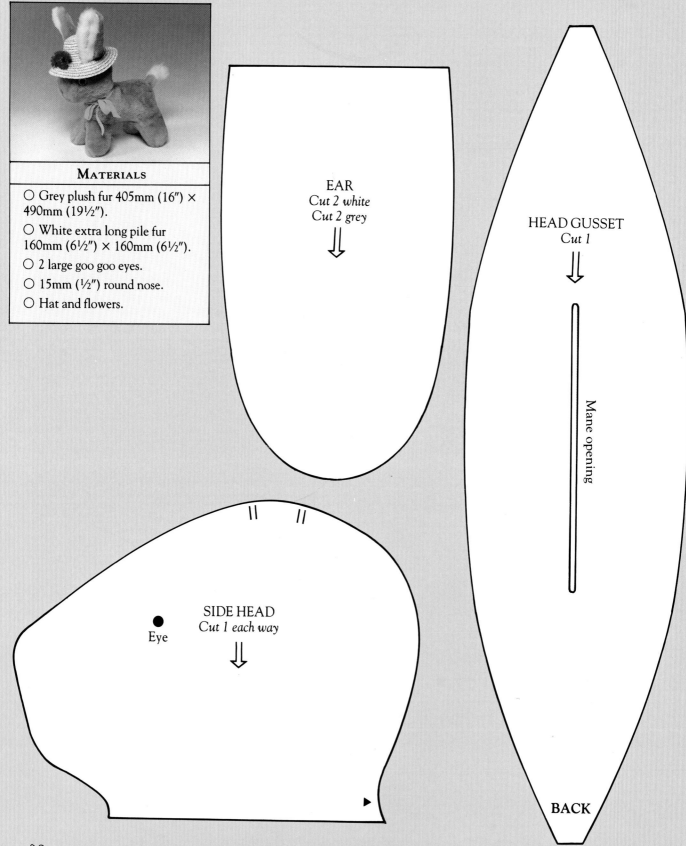

MATERIALS

○ Grey plush fur 405mm (16″) × 490mm (19½″).

○ White extra long pile fur 160mm (6½″) × 160mm (6½″).

○ 2 large goo goo eyes.

○ 15mm (½″) round nose.

○ Hat and flowers.

EAR
Cut 2 white
Cut 2 grey
⇓

HEAD GUSSET
Cut 1
⇓

Mane opening

SIDE HEAD
Cut 1 each way
⇓

Eye

▶

BACK

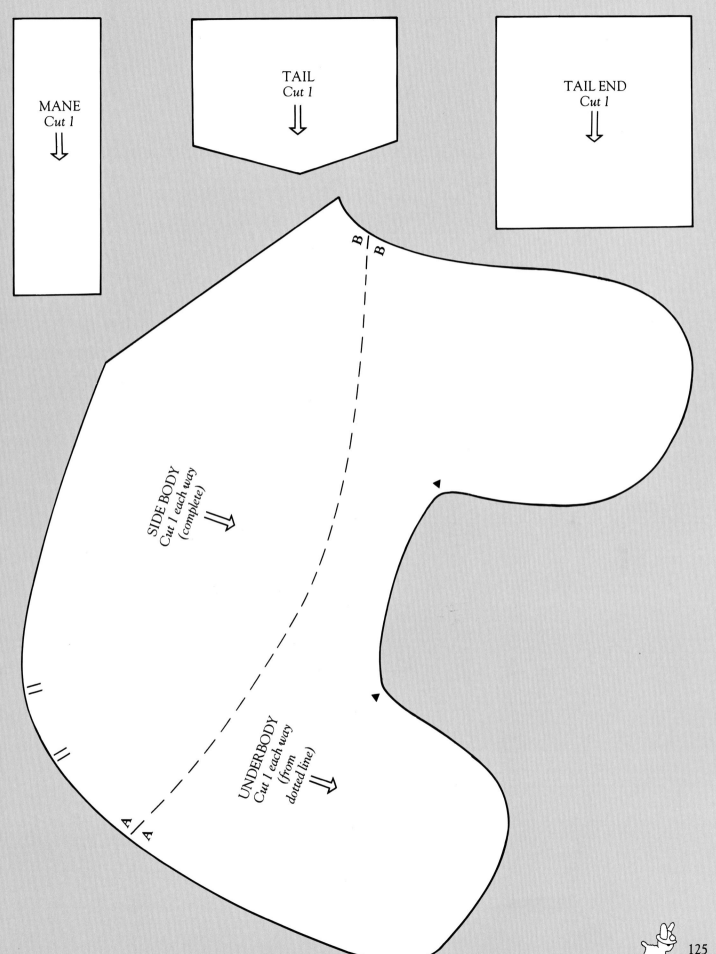

MANE
Cut 1
⇓

TAIL
Cut 1
⇓

TAIL END
Cut 1
⇓

SIDE BODY
Cut 1 each way
(complete)
⇒

UNDERBODY
Cut 1 each way
(from
dotted line)
⇒

B
B

A
A

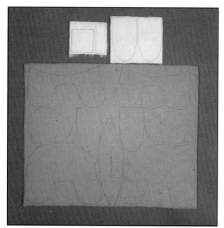

1 Make a pattern (see p.5) and draw around it on the wrong side of the fabric as shown.

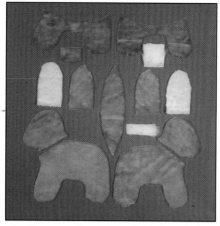

2 Cut out all pieces and check with the picture that all the sections are there.

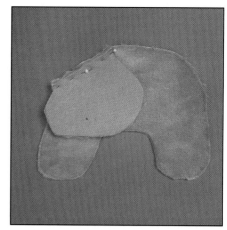

3 Pin head to body.

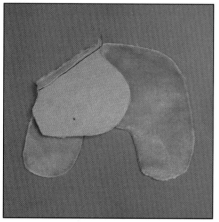

4 Sew head to body. Repeat steps **3-4** for second side.

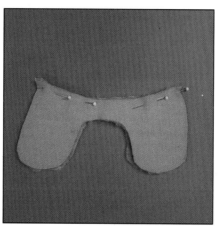

5 Place underbodies, right side facing together. Pin leaving an opening as shown for turning and stuffing.

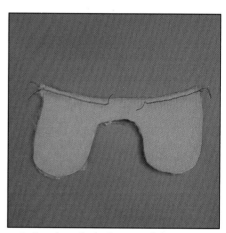

6 Stitch underbodies together.

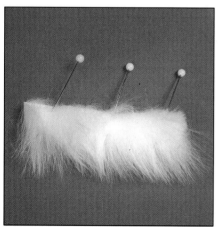

7 Pin mane in half lengthways, wrong side facing.

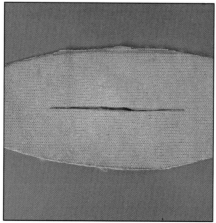

8 Cut opening in head gusset at mark as shown.

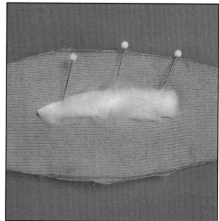

9 Insert pinned mane into opening.

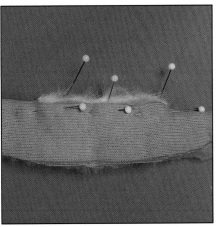

10 Fold head gusset as shown and pin.

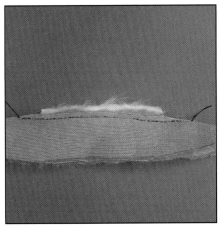

11 Carefully stitch into place, tapering off ends.

12 Open out head gusset and brush carefully.

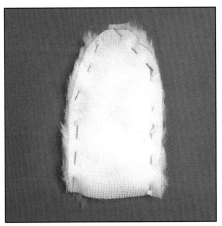

13 Place white inner ear on grey outer ear, right sides facing. Pin.

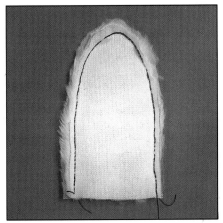

14 Stitch round ear. Repeat steps *13-14* for the other ear.

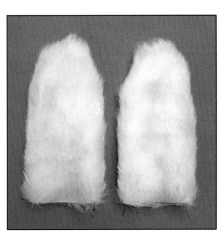

15 Turn right side out and brush.

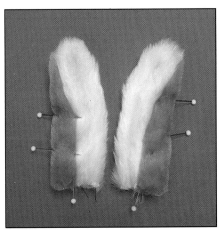

16 Pin ears over as shown.

17 Pin white end of tail to grey tail as shown.

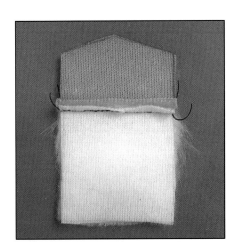

18 Stitch seam and open out tail. Brush carefully.

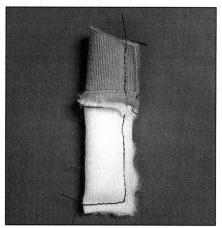

19 *Fold tail in half lengthways. Pin and stitch leaving grey end open as shown.*

20 *Turn tail right side out and brush gently.*

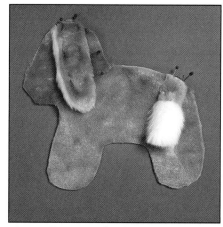

21 *Pin ear and tail in position on the side of the body as shown.*

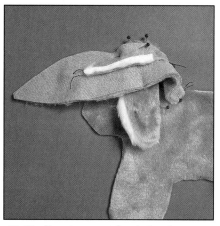

22 *Starting at neck, pin head gusset round to the top of the head and then continue past the nose down to the chin.*

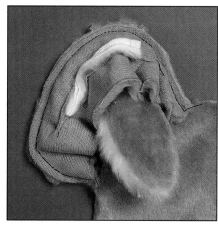

23 *Stitch round head carefully. Pin ear on second side of body as in step 21.*

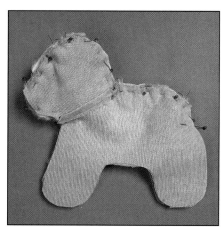

24 *Place second side of body on top of the first side, right sides together. Pin from point A to point B as shown.*

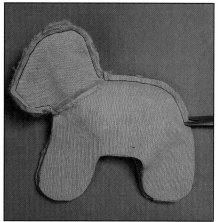

25 *Stitch along seam line, carefully snipping stitching to seam at points A and B as shown.*

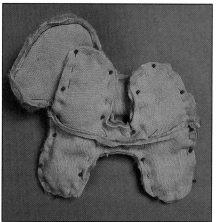

26 *Open up legs. Place underbody on top, right sides together, and pin in place.*

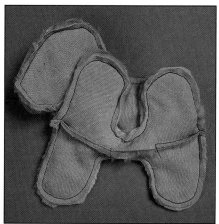

27 *Stitch carefully as shown.*

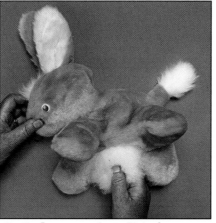

28 *Insert eyes (see p.8). Gently turn right side out by easing head through opening in underbody and continuing with the legs. Brush all seams.*

29 *Insert nose (see p.8) in the chosen place. Stuff the head, legs and then the body with sufficient stuffing to achieve a firm, but not hard, shape.*

30 *Close the opening with ladder stitch (see p.8). Pull thread up tightly and secure. Brush gently all over. Decorate with a hat and bow of your choice.*

HENRIETTA the HEN ☆☆☆

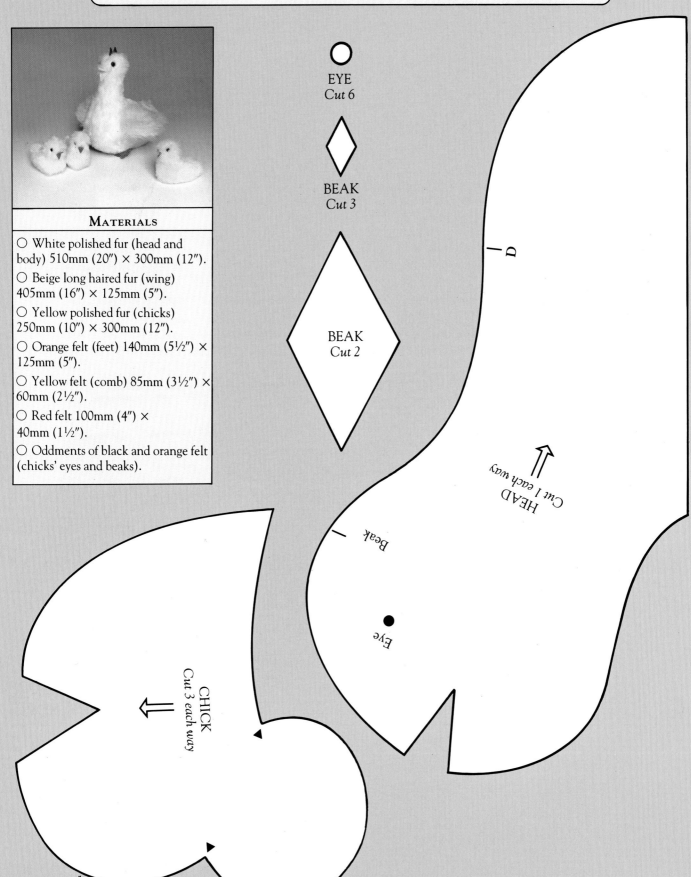

MATERIALS

○ White polished fur (head and body) 510mm (20″) × 300mm (12″).

○ Beige long haired fur (wing) 405mm (16″) × 125mm (5″).

○ Yellow polished fur (chicks) 250mm (10″) × 300mm (12″).

○ Orange felt (feet) 140mm (5½″) × 125mm (5″).

○ Yellow felt (comb) 85mm (3½″) × 60mm (2½″).

○ Red felt 100mm (4″) × 40mm (1½″).

○ Oddments of black and orange felt (chicks' eyes and beaks).

EYE
Cut 6

BEAK
Cut 3

BEAK
Cut 2

D

HEAD
Cut 1 each way

Beak

Eye

CHICK
Cut 3 each way

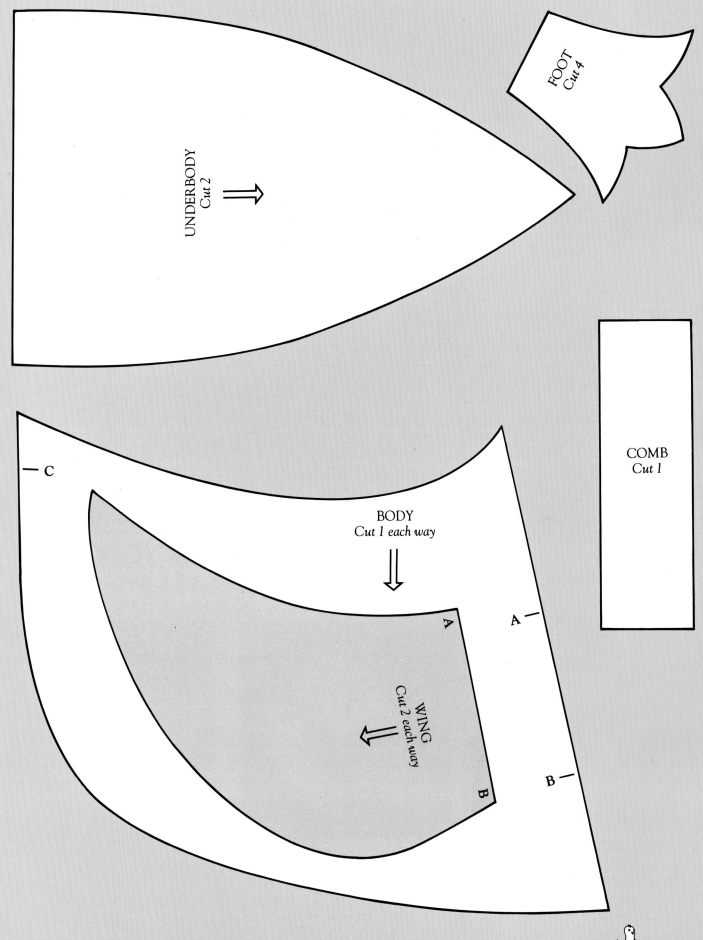

FOOT
Cut 4

UNDERBODY
Cut 2

COMB
Cut 1

— C

BODY
Cut 1 each way

A —

A

WING
Cut 2 each way

B —

B

131

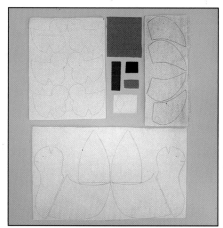

1 Make a pattern (see p.5) and draw around it on the wrong side of the fabric as shown.

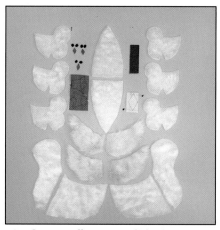

2 Cut out all pieces and check with the picture that all the sections are there.

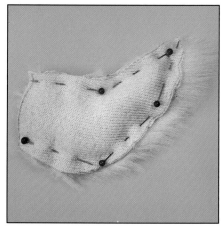

3 Pin together the wings with right sides of material facing.

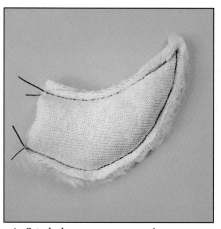

4 Stitch the two pieces together.

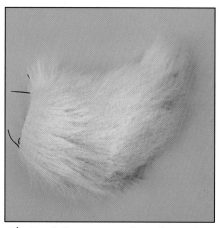

5 Carefully turn wing through to right side. Push out top with blunt end of pencil. Brush seam. Repeat steps *3-5* for second wing.

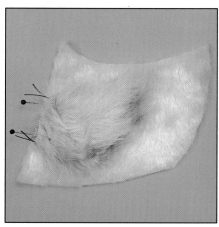

6 Place wings on body, matching **A** and **B**.

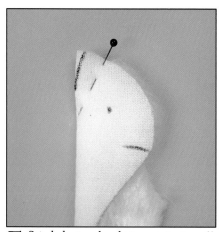

7 Stitch dart on head piece, tapering off end.

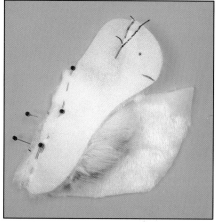

8 Place head piece on to body and wing, right sides together, then pin as shown.

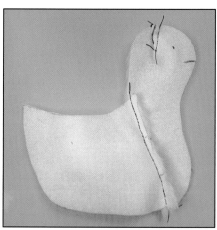

9 Stitch pieces together. Repeat steps *6-9* for second side.

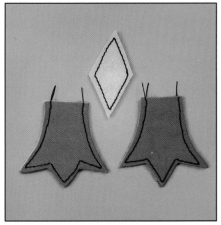

10 *Sew round feet. Cut out and lightly stuff. Sew around beak.*

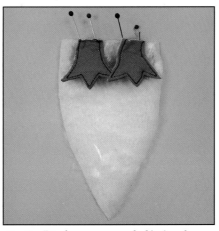

11 *Pin feet on to one half of underbody, with right side of material upwards.*

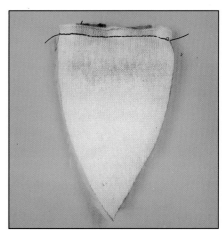

12 *Place second side of underbody to first side, right sides facing. Pin and stitch. Open out and brush seam.*

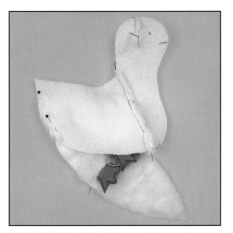

13 *With right sides together and starting at* **C**, *pin underbody to body finishing at* **D**.

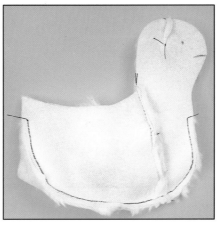

14 *Stitch as shown. Snip to seam line at* **C** *and* **D**.

15 *Place the red felt comb on top of the head (right side of material facing upwards). Pin as shown.*

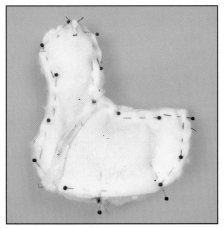

16 *Place second side on top of first, right sides together. Pin, leaving opening at bottom by feet.*

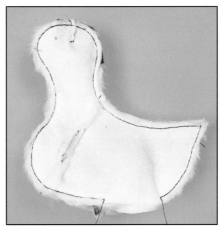

17 *Stitch the two pieces together.*

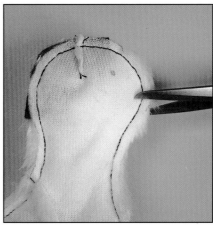

18 *Cut opening for beak where indicated.*

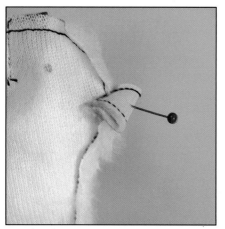

19 Fold beak in half and insert beak into opening, point first. Pin.

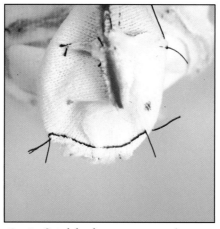

20 Stitch beak in position as shown, tapering off at sides.

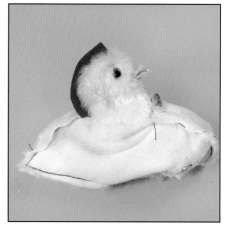

21 Insert eyes (see p.8). Gently turn right side out through opening in base.

22 Stuff with sufficient filling to achieve a firm, but not hard, result.

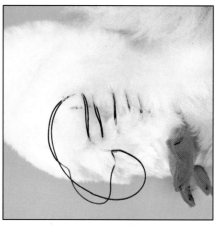

23 Close opening with ladder stitch (see p.8). Pull up thread tightly and secure.

24 Brush all seams.

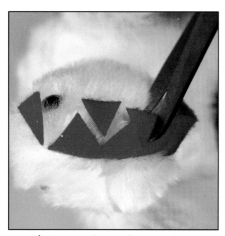

25 Cut comb into shape as shown.

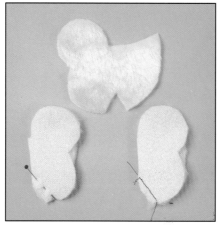

26 Sew dart on chicks as shown.

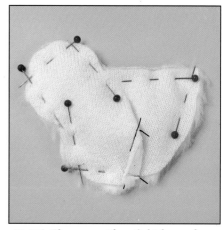

27 Place two sides of chick together with right sides facing. Pin leaving small opening in base.

28 Stitch round. Snip at corners taking care not to cut stitching. Turn right side out. Brush seams.

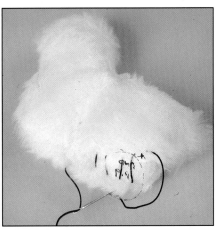

29 Stuff the chicks with sufficient filling to achieve a firm but not hard result. Close opening with ladder stitch and secure.

30 Sew on felt beaks and circles of black felt for eyes. Brush all over.

TIMOTHY the TIGER CUB ☆☆☆

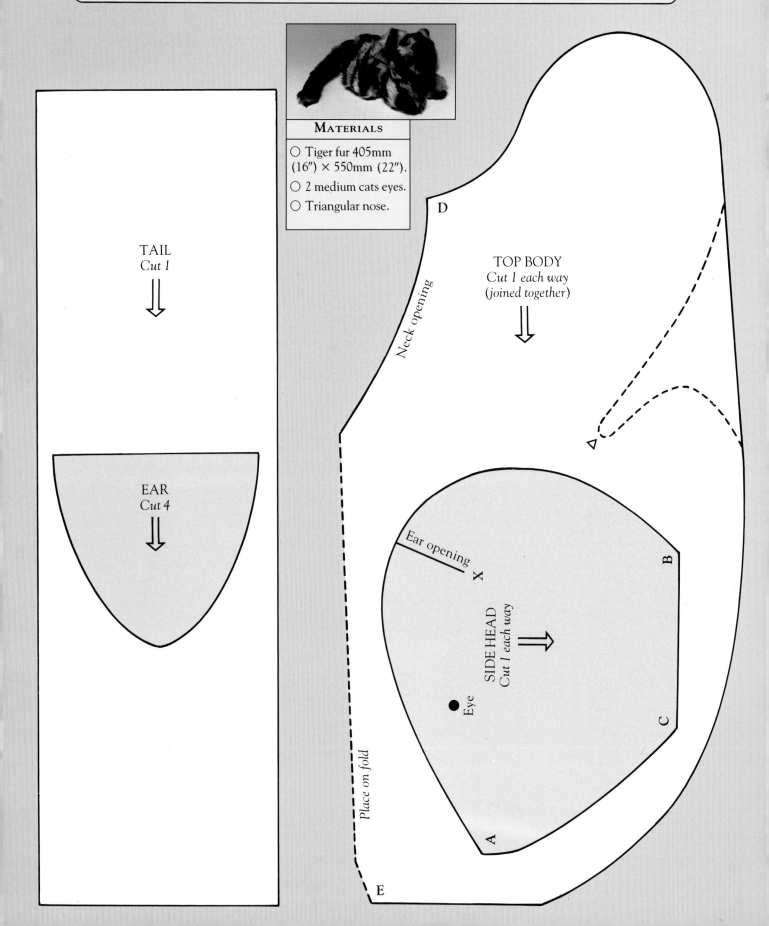

MATERIALS

○ Tiger fur 405mm
(16″) × 550mm (22″).

○ 2 medium cats eyes.

○ Triangular nose.

TAIL
Cut 1
⇩

EAR
Cut 4
⇩

TOP BODY
Cut 1 each way
(joined together)
⇩

D

Neck opening

▷

SIDE HEAD
Cut 1 each way
⇨

Ear opening

X

B

● Eye

C

Place on fold

A

E

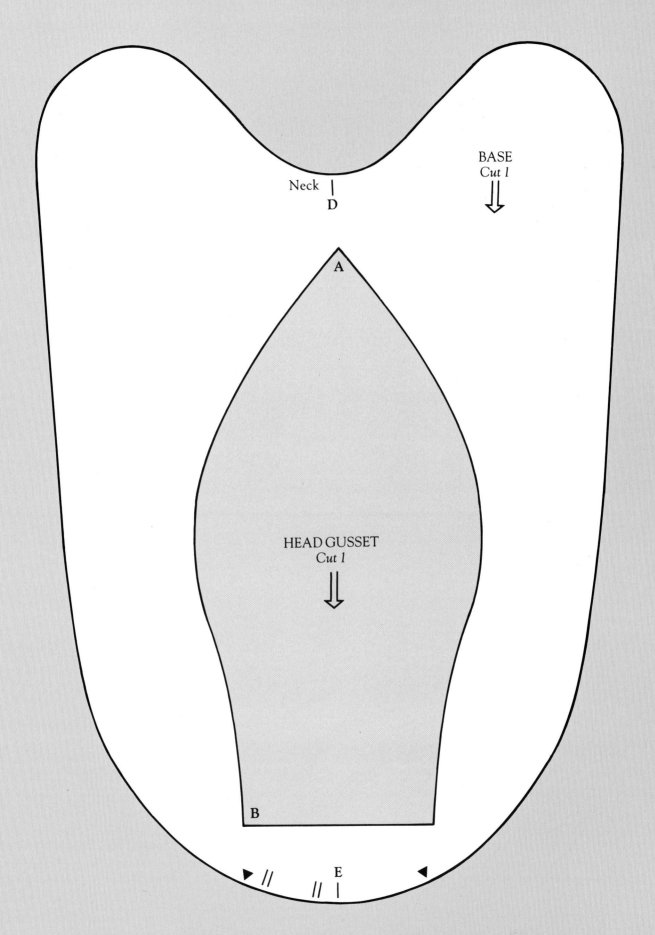

BASE
Cut 1
⇓

Neck |
D

A

HEAD GUSSET
Cut 1
⇓

B

▶ // // E | ◀

1 *Make a pattern (see p.5) and carefully place on wrong side of fabric, ensuring that a dark line runs down the centre back and tail. Draw round all pattern pieces.*

2 *Cut out all pieces and check with the picture that all the sections are there.*

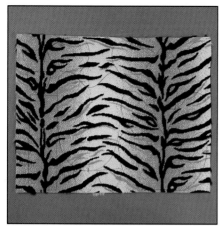

3 *Pin ears together, right sides facing.*

4 *Stitch round ears leaving bottom open. Turn right side out. Brush seams.*

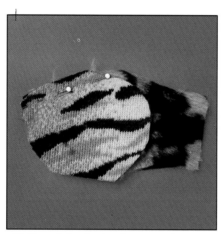

5 *Pin side head to head gusset as shown, starting at* **A** *and ending at* **B**.

6 *Carefully stitch side head to head gusset.*

7 *Pin second side to first matching* **B** *to* **C**, *leaving neck open.*

8 *Stitch in place.*

9 *Starting at* **X** *on side head, carefully cut ear opening across top of head gusset and down to* **X** *on second side head.*

10 Insert ears into ear opening and pin into place. Pin seam from **X** to **X**.

11 Stitch ear opening seam, tapering off ends. Insert eyes (see p. 10).

12 Gently turn head right side out and insert nose. Brush seams.

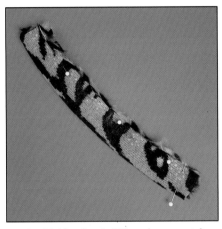

13 Fold tail in half lengthways, right side together, leaving one end open.

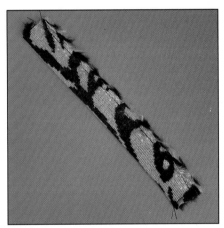

14 Stitch.

15 Carefully turn tail right side out using the blunt end of a knitting needle. Brush seam.

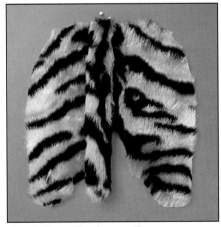

16 Pin tail to base at **E**.

17 Fold base in half. Pin across to hold tail in place as shown.

18 Stitch. Carefully cut to stitching line at easing points.

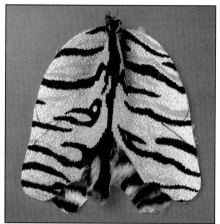

19 *Matching points at* **D** *and* **E***, place body on base, right sides together.*

20 *Carefully pin round body, starting at* **D** *(leaving neck open) and work towards tail* **E***. (Follow the stitching line.)*

21 *Pin second side to match first, leaving neck open at* **D***.*

22 *Stitch round body leaving neck open.*

23 *With sharp scissors carefully cut away fabric leaving seam allowance as shown.*

24 *Turn right side out.*

25 *Brush all seams and ease out any fur which has been trapped.*

26 *Starting with paws, stuff with sufficient filling to achieve a firm but not hard result.*

27 *Finish stuffing body.*

28 With stranded cotton embroider a friendly mouth under nose as shown. Stuff head with sufficient filling to achieve a firm result.

29 Matching head carefully to body, join firmly with ladder stitch (see p.8). Pull thread up tightly and secure.

30 With sharp scissors carefully trim a little of the fur away from around the nose as shown. Brush gently all over. Finish with a ribbon bow.

GERALD *the* HOT TEDDY ☆☆☆

MATERIALS
○ Honey Polished Fur 610mm × 510mm (24″ × 20″)
○ Red Polished Fur 305mm × 404mm (12″ × 16″)
○ Cotton Lining 205mm × 205mm (8″ × 8″)
○ 2 Small Teddy Eyes
○ 1 Flocked Nose

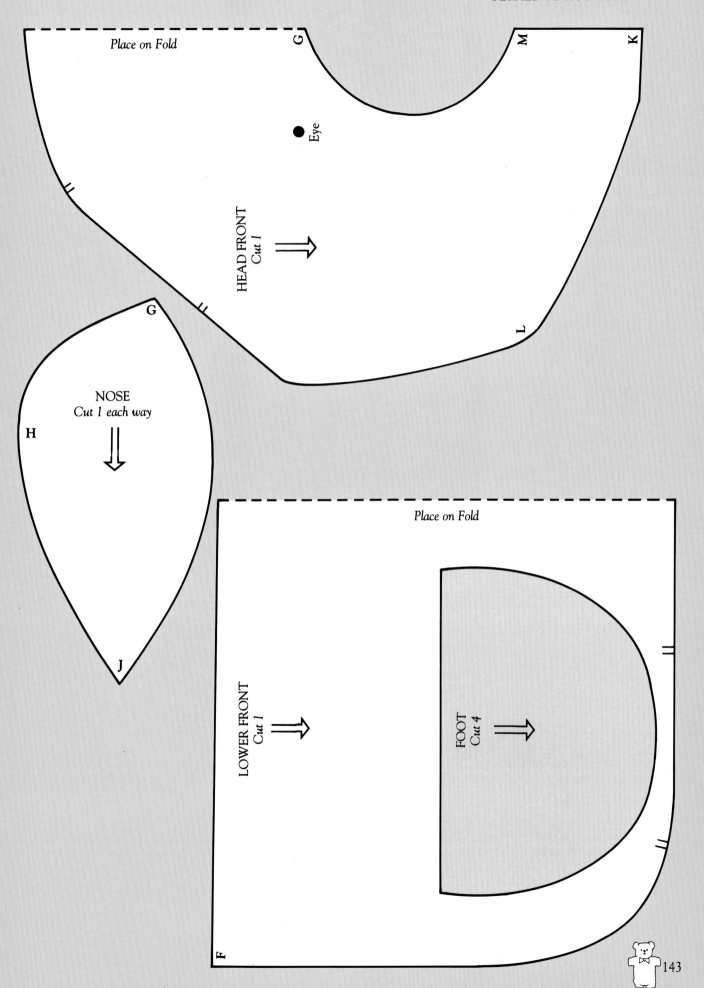

Place on Fold

G   M   K

● Eye

HEAD FRONT
Cut 1
⇒

G

NOSE
Cut 1 each way
⇓

H

J

L

Place on Fold

LOWER FRONT
Cut 1
⇒

FOOT
Cut 4
⇒

F   M

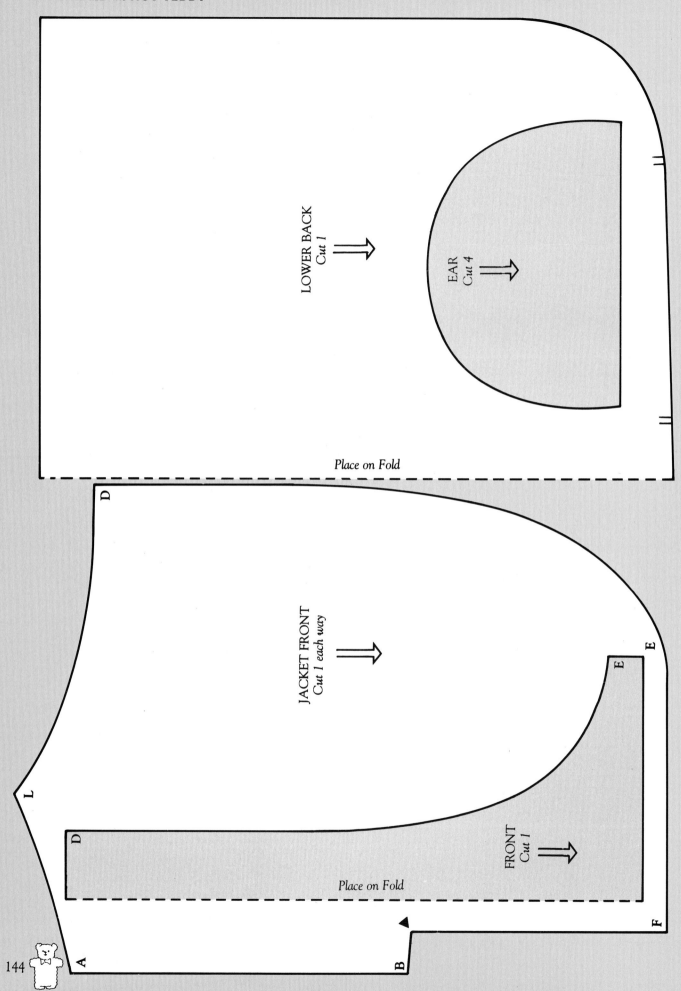

LOWER BACK
Cut 1

EAR
Cut 4

Place on Fold

JACKET FRONT
Cut 1 each way

FRONT
Cut 1

Place on Fold

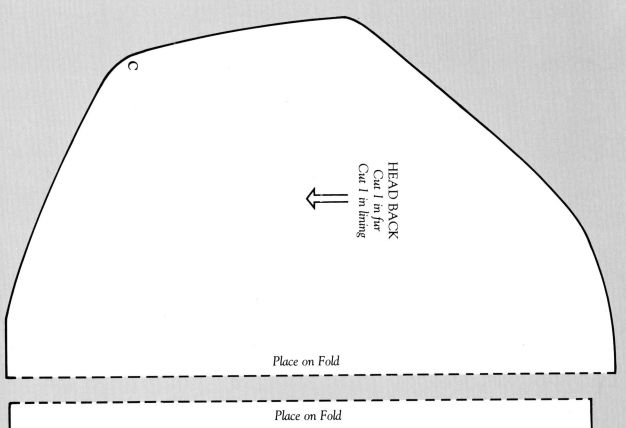

HEAD BACK
Cut 1 in fur
Cut 1 in lining

C

Place on Fold

Place on Fold

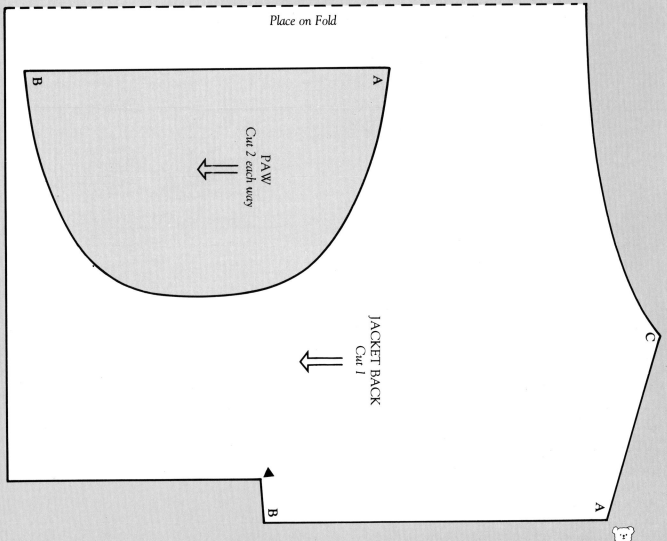

B

A

PAW
Cut 2 each way

JACKET BACK
Cut 1

C

▲

B

A

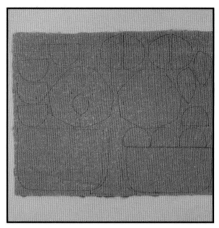

1 Make a pattern (see p.5) and draw around the appropriate pieces on the wrong side of the fur fabric, as shown.

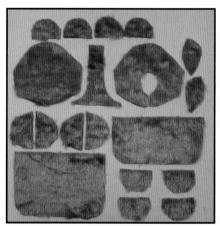

2 Draw around the appropriate pattern pieces on the wrong side of the jacket fabric. Cut the head lining from cotton fabric.

3 Cut out all the pieces from the fur fabric and check with the picture that all the sections are there.

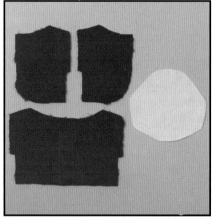

4 Cut out the jacket pieces and the cotton lining facing. Check with the picture that all the pieces are there.

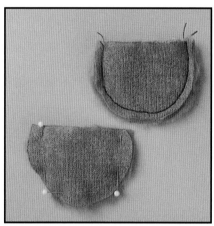

5 With right sides facing, pin and stitch the foot pieces together, leaving the straight edges open.

6 Turn the feet right side out and brush the seams.

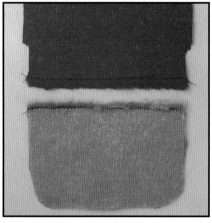

7 To make a hem along the bottom edge of the jacket and lower back, turn the seam allowances to the wrong side and secure with a zigzag stitch.

8 Pin and stitch 2 of the paws between **A** and **B** on either side of the jacket back.

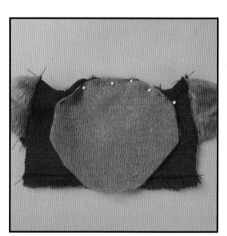

9 With right sides facing, pin the back head to jacket back, matching **C** to **C**.

10 Stitch the back head to the jacket back along the seam line.

11 Pin the remaining 2 paws between **A** and **B** on each front jacket piece.

12 Stitch the paws to the front jacket pieces along the seam lines.

13 With right sides facing, pin the front to one front jacket piece from **D** to **E**, as shown.

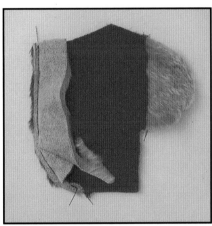

14 Stitch the front to the jacket front piece along the seam line and brush the seam.

15 With right sides facing, pin the second jacket front to the front, from **D** to **E**.

16 Stitch the second jacket front to the front along the seam line and brush the seam.

17 With right sides facing, pin the lower front along the lower edge of the front and front jacket pieces, matching **F** to **F**.

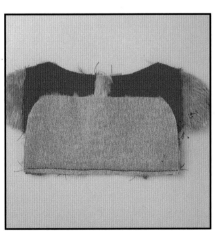

18 Stitch the lower front to the front and jacket pieces along the seam line and brush the seam.

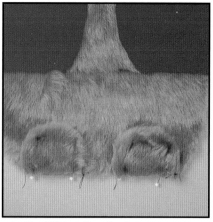

19 With right sides facing, pin the feet to the lower front in the positions marked on the template.

20 With right sides facing, pin and stitch the ear pieces together, leaving the straight edges open.

21 Turn the ears right side out and brush the seams.

22 With right sides facing, pin the nose pieces together from **H** to **H**.

23 Stitch the nose pieces together along the seam line, and brush the seam.

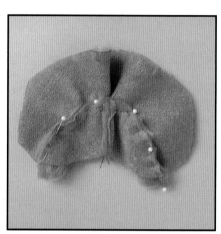

24 Open out the nose and, with right sides facing, pin it to the head from **G** to **J** and **J** to **G**.

25 Stitch the nose to the head along the seam line and brush the seam.

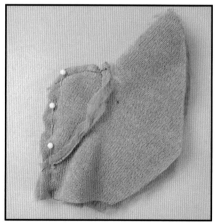

26 With right sides facing, fold the head in half and pin the nose from **H**, matching **J** to **K**.

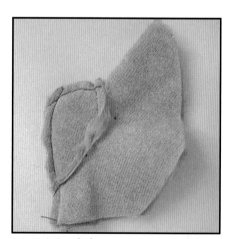

27 Stitch the remaining part of the nose along the seam line and brush the seam.

28 *Brush all the seams. Insert the eyes and nose, and embroider the mouth (see p.8).*

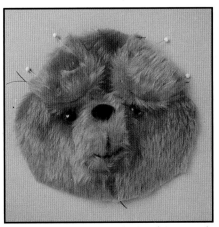

29 *Pin the ears to the head front in the positions marked on the template.*

30 *With right sides facing, pin the front head to the front body, matching L to L.*

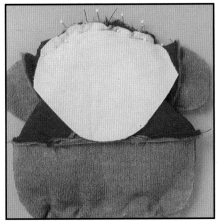

31 *Turn the body over. Pin the cotton lining to the front from L to L, catching in the body between the 2 head layers, as shown.*

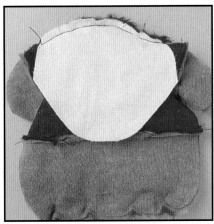

32 *Stitch the cotton head lining to the front along the seam line. Check that the body is secured in the stitching line. Brush the seam.*

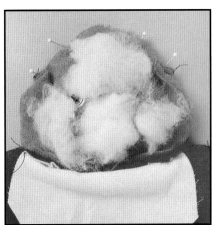

33 *Stuff the nose, and lightly stuff the front of the face, with the filling.*

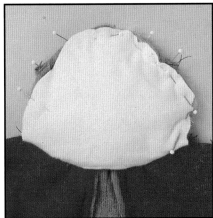

34 *Fold the cotton lining over the back of the face and pin it into position.*

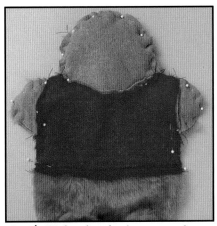

35 *With right sides facing, pin the jacket back over the front body, as shown.*

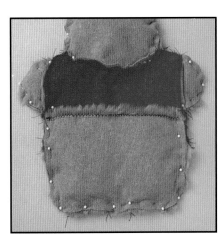

36 *With right sides facing, pin the lower back over the front. Keep the bottom edges even so that it overlaps the jacket back.*

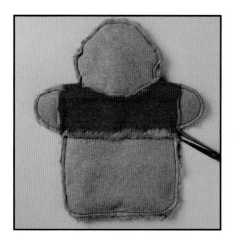

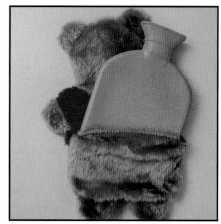

37 Stitch around the whole body. Snip the seams at the ease points.

38 Turn the teddy right side out and brush the seams.

39 Insert a hot water bottle through the opening in the back. Complete the teddy by attaching a bow of ribbon to its neck.

MARVIN the MONKEY ☆☆☆☆

MATERIALS

○ White Long Fur 510mm (20″) × 350mm (14″).

○ Brown Polished Fur 250mm (10″) × 205mm (8″).

○ Felt for jacket 300mm (12″) × 150mm (6″).

○ 2 Small Teddy Eyes.

○ 1 Small Ball Nose.

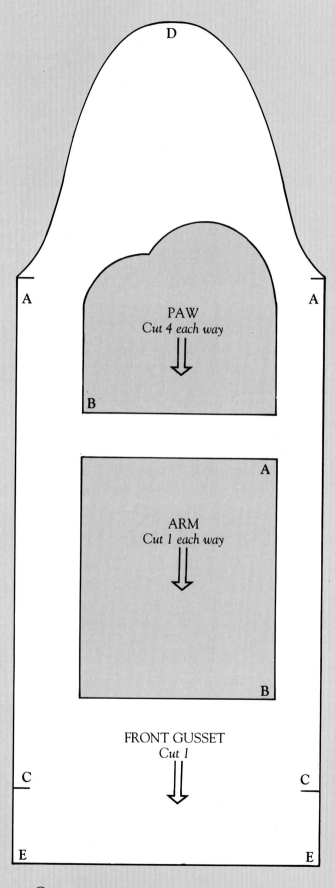

D

A   A

PAW
Cut 4 each way
⇓

B

A

ARM
Cut 1 each way
⇓

B

FRONT GUSSET
Cut 1
⇓

C   C

E   E

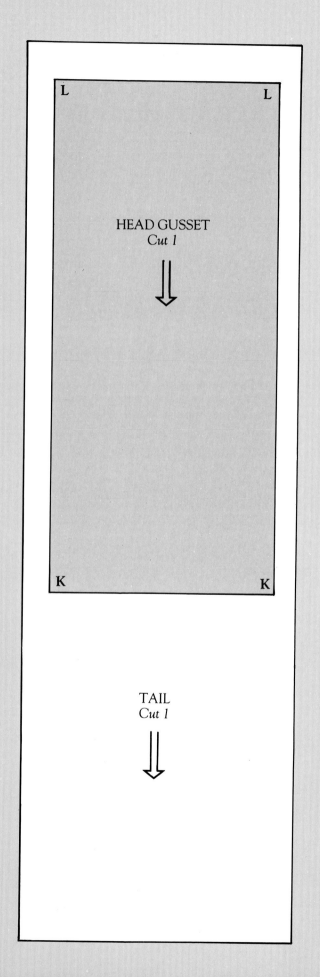

L   L

HEAD GUSSET
Cut 1
⇓

K   K

TAIL
Cut 1
⇓

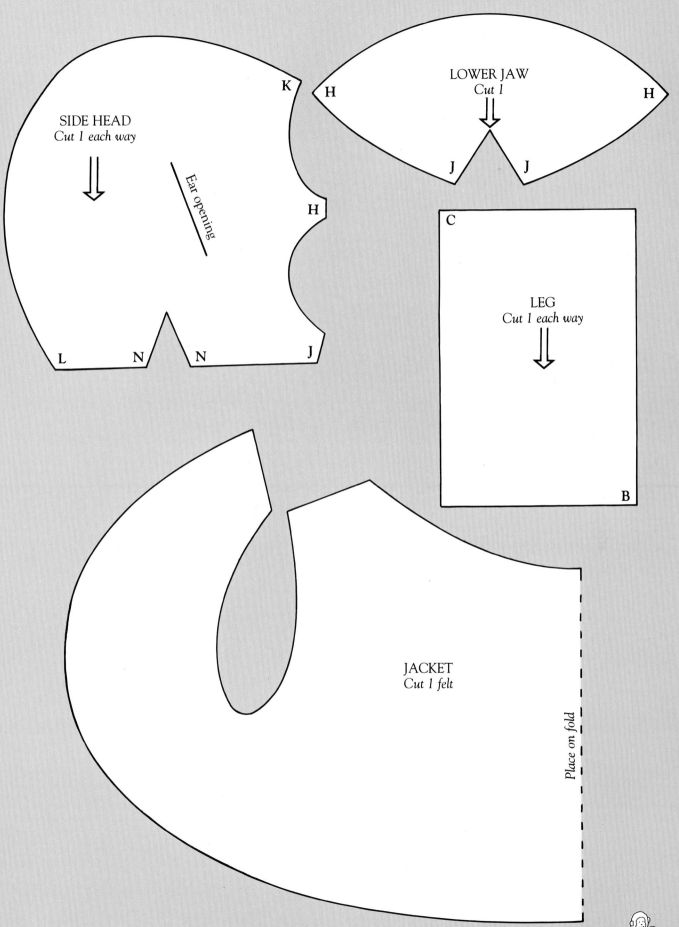

SIDE HEAD
Cut 1 each way

Ear opening

K

H

H

J

L   N   N   J

LOWER JAW
Cut 1

H

H

J   J

LEG
Cut 1 each way

C

B

JACKET
Cut 1 felt

Place on fold

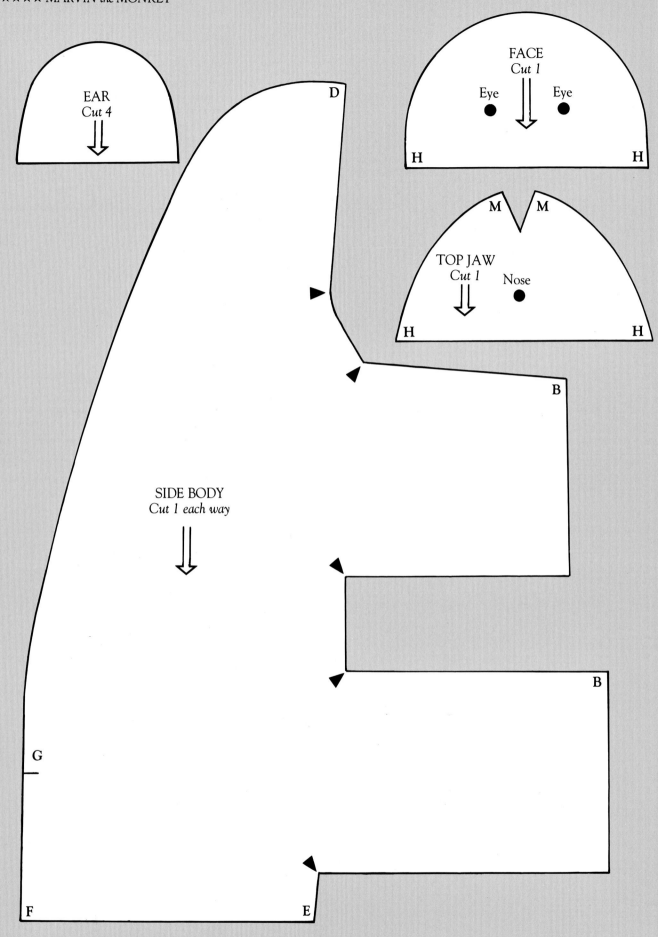

EAR
Cut 4

FACE
Cut 1

Eye   Eye

H   H

TOP JAW
Cut 1   Nose

M   M

H   H

D

B

SIDE BODY
Cut 1 each way

B

G

F   E

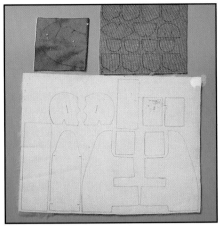

1 Make a pattern of each template shape required (see p.5). Then draw around each pattern on the wrong side of the appropriate material, as shown.

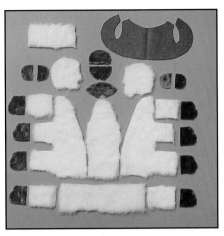

2 Cut out all pieces and then check with the picture that all the sections are there.

3 Pin **M** to **M** on top jaw, to form a dart.

4 Stitch dart together tapering off the ends. Open out to form the top jaw.

5 Pin top jaw to straight edge of face, right sides facing, matching **H** to **H**.

6 Stitch seam from **H** to **H**. Unfold and brush seams.

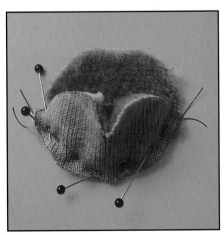

7 Pin lower jaw to top jaw, right sides facing, from **H** to **H**.

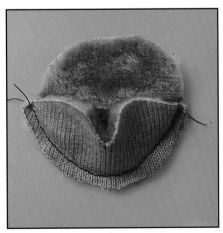

8 Stitch the seam from **H** to **H**, to complete the face.

9 Turn the face right side out and brush all seams.

10 Pin ear pieces together, right sides facing.

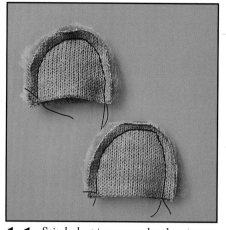

11 Stitch the pieces together leaving bottom edge open, as shown.

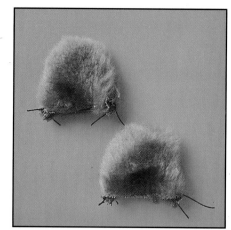

12 Turn each ear right side out and brush the seams.

13 Push an ear into a side head opening, leaving open end showing.

14 Fold the side head along the opening, right sides facing, and then pin together to secure the ear.

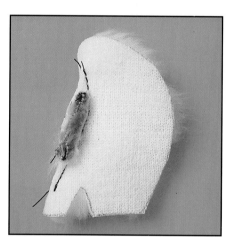

15 Carefully stitch into place, tapering off stitching as shown.

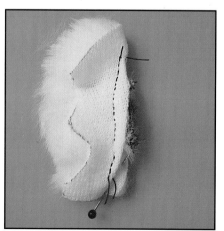

16 Pin dart together at position marked **N**.

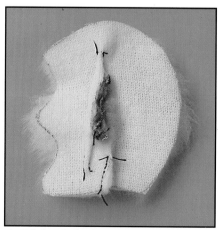

17 Stitch the dart, tapering off the seam. Repeat steps 13-17 for second side head.

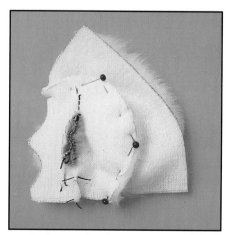

18 Pin side head to head gusset from **K** to **K**, as shown.

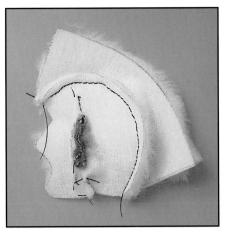

19 *Using seam allowance carefully stitch from L to K.*

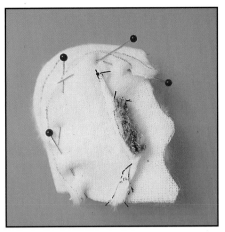

20 *Turn head over and then pin second side head to gusset from K to L.*

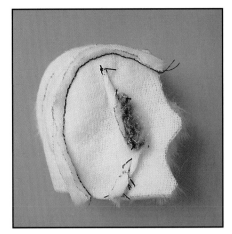

21 *Using seam allowance carefully stitch from L to K.*

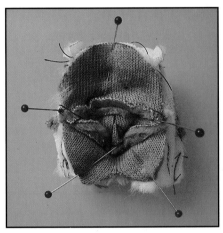

22 *Place face into head, right sides facing, match and pin positions J, H and top centre of face.*

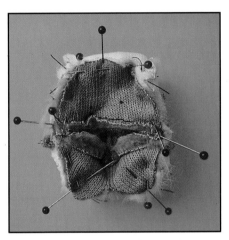

23 *Very carefully further pin face to head between the first pins, as shown.*

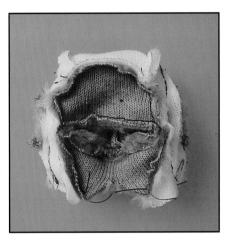

24 *Stitch face to head from J to J, leaving the neck open.*

25 *Place J to J on the lower jaw to form a dart, then pin in position.*

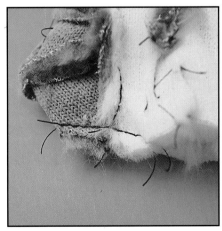

26 *Stitch the dart as shown. Insert safety eyes and nose. Turn right side out.*

27 *Brush head well. Stitch on a mouth (see p.8) as shown. Stuff front of head firmly.*

28 Pin a paw to an arm, matching at **B**. Repeat for second arm.

29 Stitch along the seam line. Repeat steps 28-29 for legs.

30 Picture shows the arms and legs with paws correctly attached.

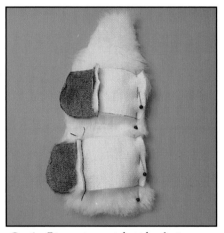

31 Pin an arm, right sides facing, at **A** on the front gusset. Then pin a leg at **C**.

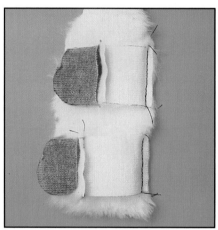

32 Stitch the arm and leg to the gusset as shown.

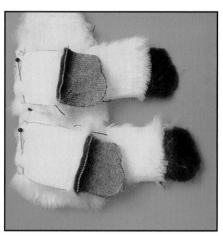

33 Repeat step 31 for the opposite arm and leg.

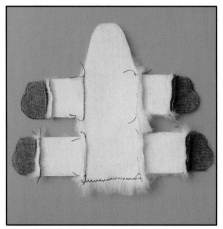

34 Stitch the arm and leg to gusset to complete the front. Turn up bottom edge and sew with zigzag stitch.

35 Pin paws to side body, right sides together, at **B**.

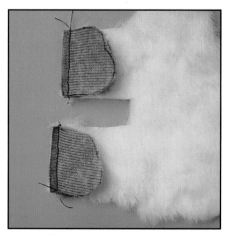

36 Stitch the paws into place. Repeat steps 35-36 for second side.

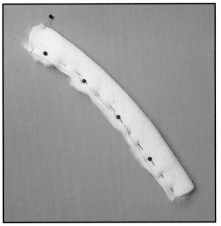

37 Fold tail in half, right sides facing, and pin along side and one end.

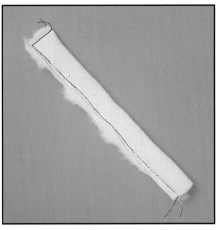

38 Using seam allowance stitch the tail, as shown.

39 Turn the tail right side out and brush the seam.

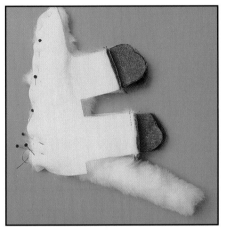

40 Pin tail to side body at position **G**. Place second side, right sides facing, to first and pin from **F** to **D**.

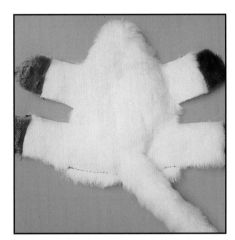

41 Stitch from **D** to **F**. Unfold body and turn up seam allowance, along bottom edge, and sew with zigzag stitch. Brush the seams.

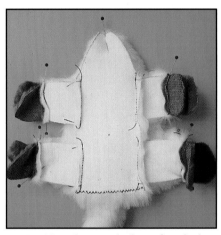

42 Place front on body, right sides facing, pin matching at positions **B** and **D**.

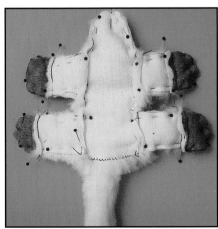

43 Continue pinning around body from **E** to **E**.

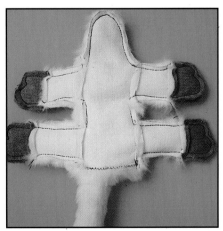

44 Carefully stitch body together from **E** to **E**, leaving bottom edge open.

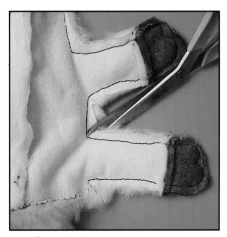

45 With sharp scissors, cut seam allowance to the stitching line at all ease points.

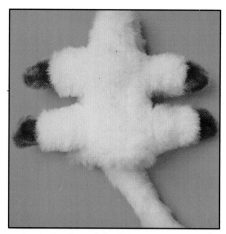

46 Push each limb into centre of body and turn right side out. Brush all over.

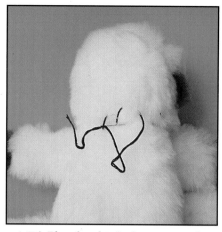

47 Place hand in body, insert neck into head. Pin and then sew head to neck. Secure the thread tightly.

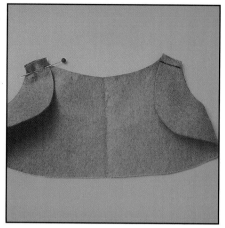

48 Pin, then stitch, each shoulder seam on the jacket. Turn right side out and dress Marvin.

GERRY the GIRAFFE ☆☆☆☆

MATERIALS

○ Ocelot fur 510mm (20") × 610mm (24").

○ Fawn felt (mane) 200mm (8") × 60mm (2½").

○ Black felt (horns and tail) 250mm (10") × 50mm (2").

○ 2 medium round black eyes.

○ Medium animal nose.

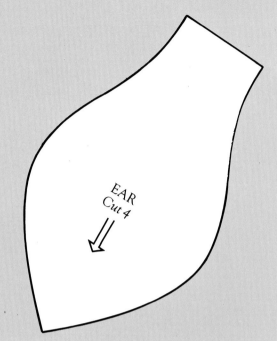

EAR
Cut 4
⇓

TAIL
Cut 1

HORNS
Cut 1

MANE
Cut 1

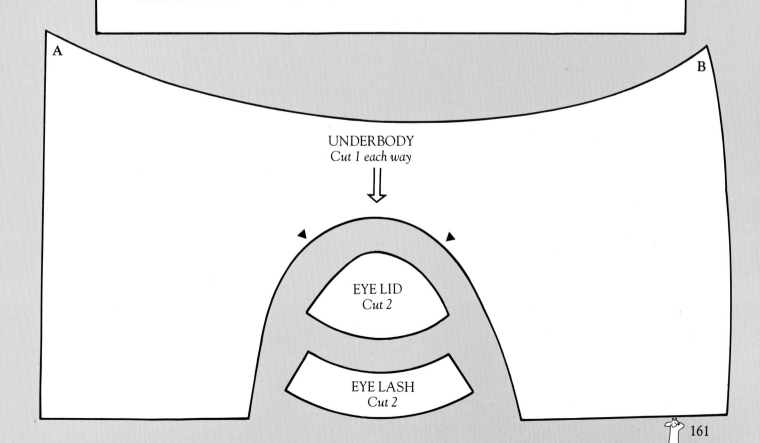

A

B

UNDERBODY
Cut 1 each way
⇓

EYE LID
Cut 2

EYE LASH
Cut 2

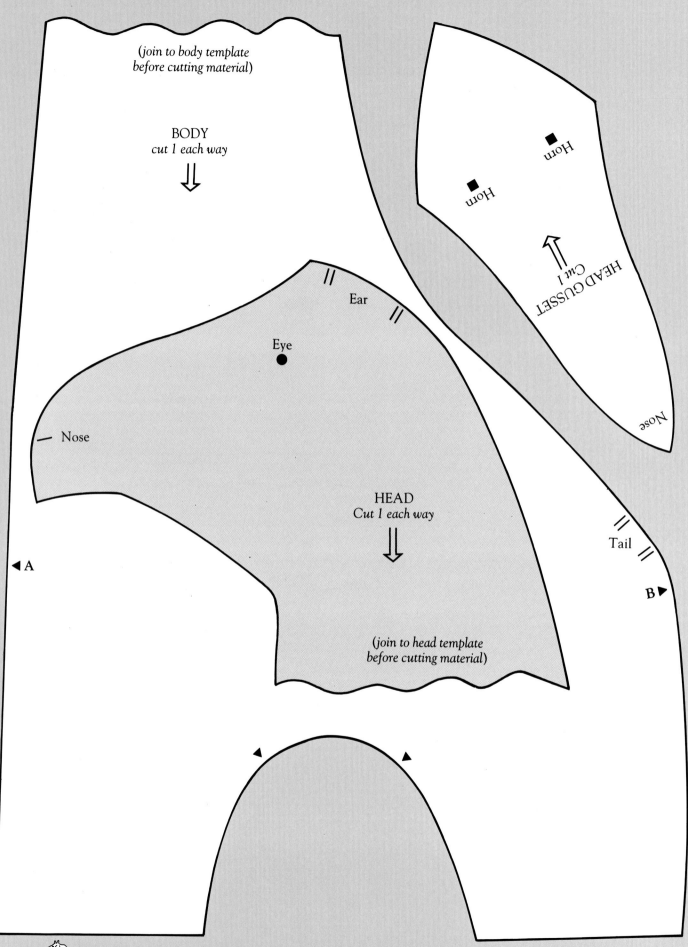

☆☆☆☆ GERRY the GIRAFFE

(join to body template
before cutting material)

BODY
cut 1 each way
⇓

Horn

Horn

HEAD GUSSET
Cut 1
⇑

Nose

Ear

Eye

Nose

HEAD
Cut 1 each way
⇓

Tail

◄A

B►

(join to head template
before cutting material)

1 Make a pattern (see p.5) and draw around it on the wrong side of the fabric as shown.

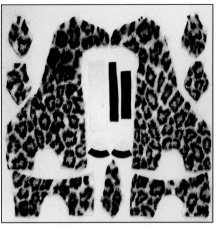

2 Cut out all pieces and check with the picture that all the sections are there.

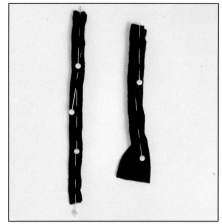

3 Fold horn in half lengthways and pin. Fold tail in half lengthways and pin leaving last 25mm (1") open as shown.

4 Stitch horn and tail. Knot one end of the horn.

5 Fringe the last 25mm (1") of tail as shown.

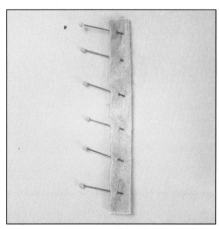

6 Fold mane in half lengthways and pin as shown.

7 Pin eyelids to eyelash as shown.

8 Carefully hand-sew lid to lash.

9 Fringe lashes as shown. Repeat steps *7-9* for second eyelid.

10 Pin eyelid on to side of head over mark for eye.

11 Stitch in place leaving lashes open. Repeat for second side head.

12 Pair ears right sides together and pin round as shown, leaving top open.

13 Stitch round ears.

14 Turn ears right side out. Brush seams.

15 Pin ears in position on head as marked.

16 Match nose on head gusset to nose on side head and pin (incorporating the ears), as shown.

17 Stitch carefully. Make a small hole at each horn mark.

18 Starting under the head gusset, pin the mane in position with folded edge to cut edge as shown. Pin tail in position.

19 *Place second side on first side, right sides facing, and pin from **A** to **B** over the head.*

20 *Stitch carefully in place. Cut to seams at **A** and **B**.*

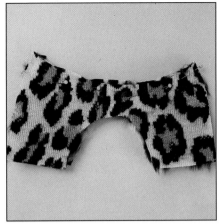

21 *Place underbodies together, right sides facing, and pin top edge, leaving opening at centre.*

22 *Stitch seam.*

23 *Open up legs and place underbody in position. Pin all the way around matching **A**'s and **B**'s.*

24 *Carefully stitch in place.*

25 *Turn right side out. Brush all seams carefully.*

26 *Insert nose in chosen position (see p.8).*

27 *Fringe mane as shown.*

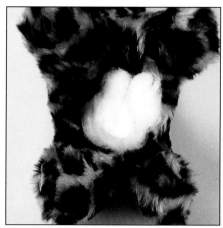

28 Insert black eye under eyelid (see p.8).

29 Insert unknotted end of horn through first hole and out through second hole. Knot end. Secure in place with small stitches.

30 Stuff with sufficient filling to achieve a firm, but not hard, result. Secure opening with ladder stitch (see p.8). Pull up and secure. Brush seams.

OSCAR *the* OSTRICH ☆☆☆☆

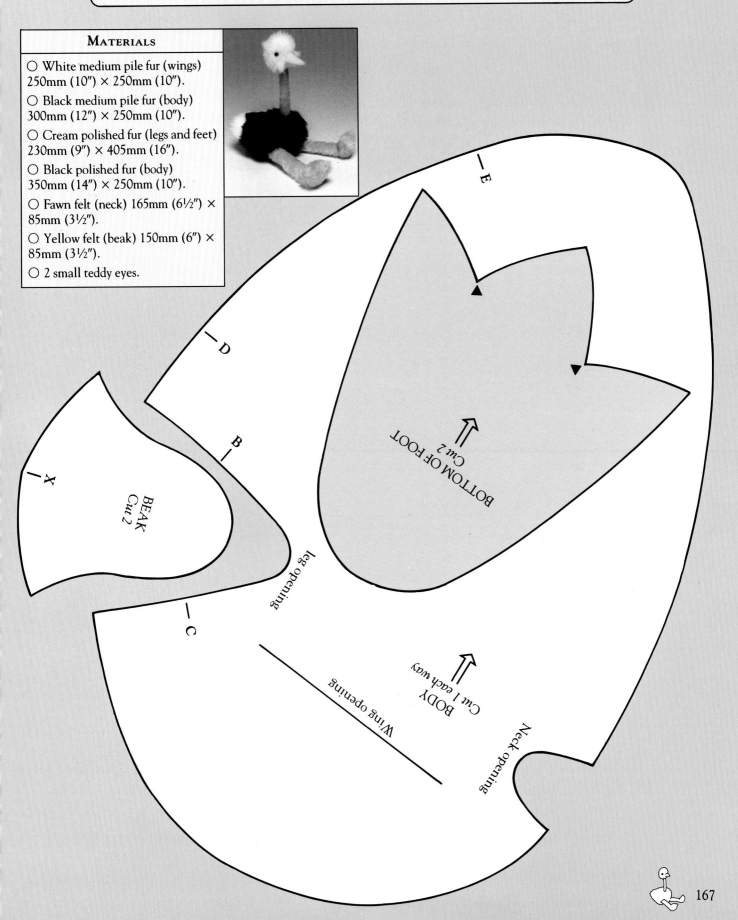

E

D

B

X

BEAK
Cut 2

C

BOTTOM OF FOOT
Cut 2

Leg opening

Wing opening

BODY
Cut 1 each way

Neck opening

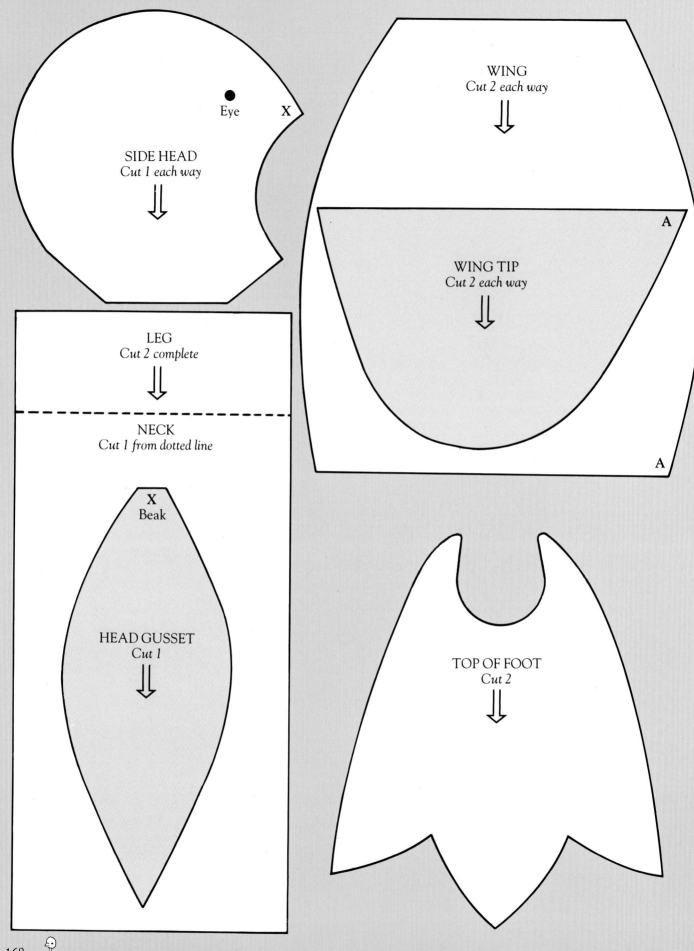

SIDE HEAD
Cut 1 each way

Eye **X**

WING
Cut 2 each way

WING TIP
Cut 2 each way

A

A

LEG
Cut 2 complete

NECK
Cut 1 from dotted line

X
Beak

HEAD GUSSET
Cut 1

TOP OF FOOT
Cut 2

1 Make a pattern (see p.5) and draw around it on the wrong side of the fabric as shown.

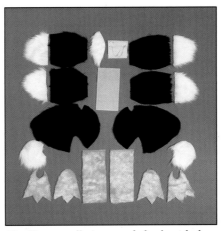

2 Cut out all pieces and check with the picture that all the sections are there.

3 Place head gusset onto side head and pin as shown.

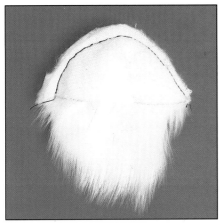

4 Sew head gusset to side head.

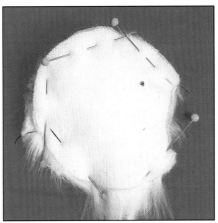

5 Place second side on top of first, right sides facing, and pin from beak hole to neck opening and from neck opening to beak hole.

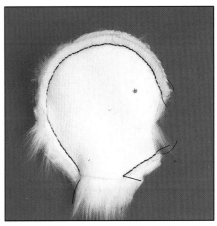

6 Stitch leaving opening for beak and neck.

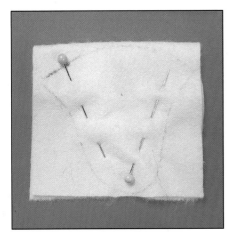

7 Pin beak pieces together.

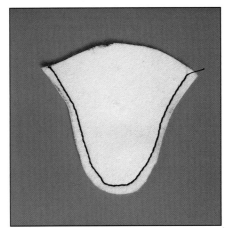

8 Stitch around beak. Cut close to stitching line as shown.

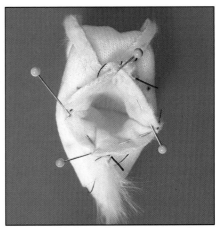

9 Insert beak into beak opening and pin in place as shown, matching at **X**.

169

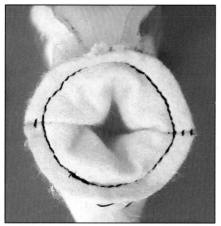

10 Carefully stitch around beak. Insert eyes at points marked (see p.8).

11 Gently turn head right side out. Brush fur fabric seams.

12 Pair feet pieces together, right sides facing inwards. Pin.

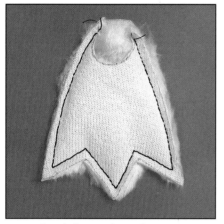

13 Stitch feet as shown leaving opening at the top. Cut to seam in corners.

14 Turn feet right side out. Brush seams.

15 Stuff head and feet with sufficient filling to achieve a firm, but not result.

16 Pin wing tip to wing, matching at **A**.

17 Stitch wing tip in place.

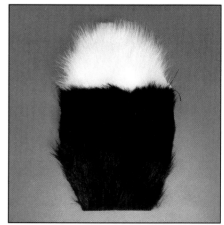

18 Open out and brush. Repeat steps *16-18* for remaining wing.

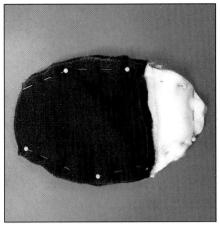

19 *Place a pair of wings together, right sides facing, and pin leaving opening at black end as shown. Stitch.*

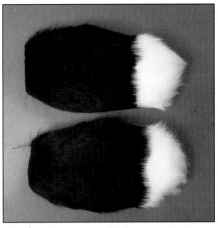

20 *Repeat step **19** for second wing. Turn wings right side out and brush seams.*

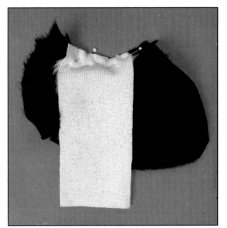

21 *Pin the top of leg to leg opening of body, starting at mark **B** and pinning to mark **C**.*

22 *Stitch leg in place.*

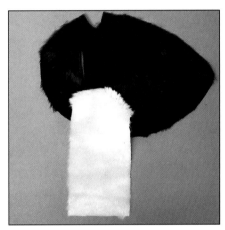

23 *Open leg out as shown. Cut wing opening.*

24 *Position wings in opening with open edge towards the front of the body. Fold over body and pin as shown.*

25 *Carefully stitch as shown, tapering off seam.*

26 *Fold leg in half and pin in place.*

27 *Stitch leg seam leaving opening at the bottom.*

28 Using the blunt end of a pencil turn leg right side out. Repeat steps *21-28* for second side.

29 Place two sides together, right sides facing, and pin from neck opening to **D**.

30 Sew as shown. Open body out right side up.

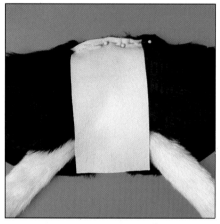

31 Place neck on neck opening and pin into place and stitch.

32 Fold neck in half and pin as shown leaving top open.

33 Continue to pin down back to **E**. Stitch seam carefully, leaving the opening.

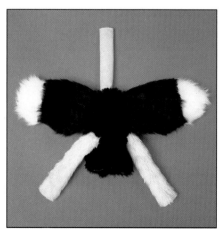

34 Very gently turn neck right side out using a suitable blunt instrument, then the body. Brush fur seams.

35 Stuff with sufficient filling to achieve a firm, but not hard result. Use the blunt end of a pencil to stuff the neck and legs very firmly.

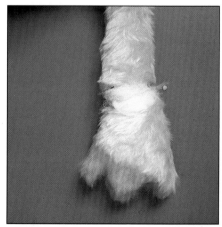

36 Pin the foot to the bottom of the leg.

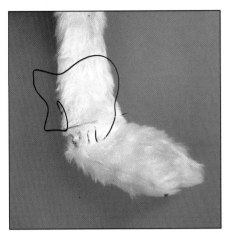

37 *Secure foot to leg with ladder stitch (see p.8) pull thread up tightly and secure. Repeat 36-37 for second foot.*

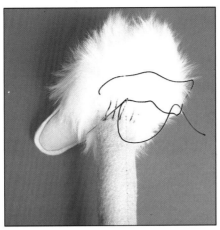

38 *Sew head securely to neck using ladder stitch. Pull thread up tightly and secure.*

39 *Close opening in body with ladder stitch. Brush lightly all fur seams. Pin wings in position and secure with small stitches.*

TINY TED ☆☆☆☆

MATERIALS
○ Gold Plush Fur 560mm × 305mm (22″ × 12″)
○ 2 Medium Teddy Eyes
○ 1 Small Heart Nose
○ 4 Small Joints
○ Ribbon 455mm (18″)

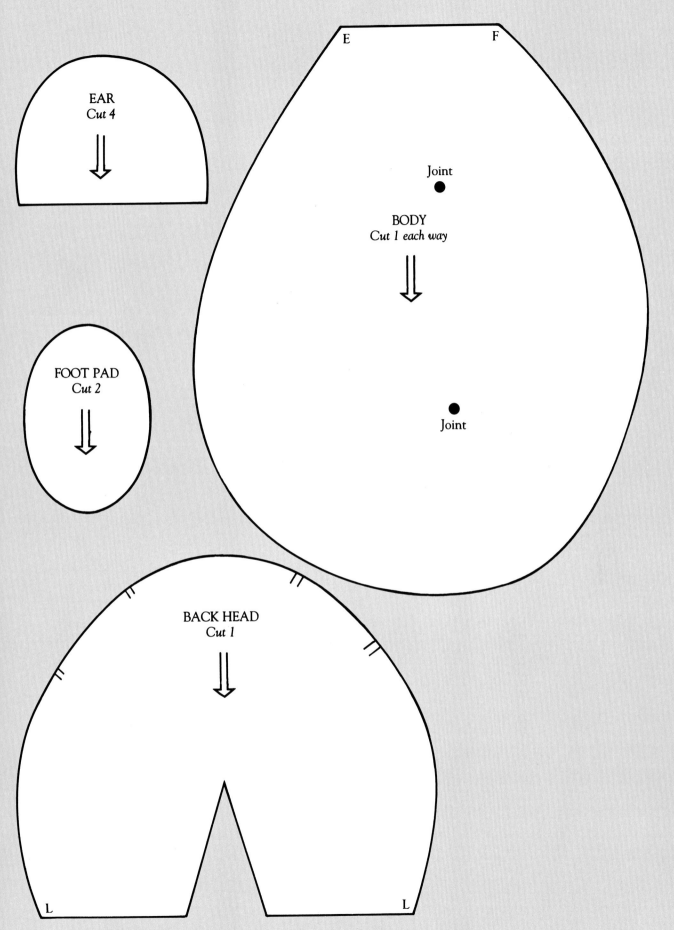

EAR
Cut 4

E   F

Joint
●

BODY
Cut 1 each way

Joint
●

FOOT PAD
Cut 2

BACK HEAD
Cut 1

L   L

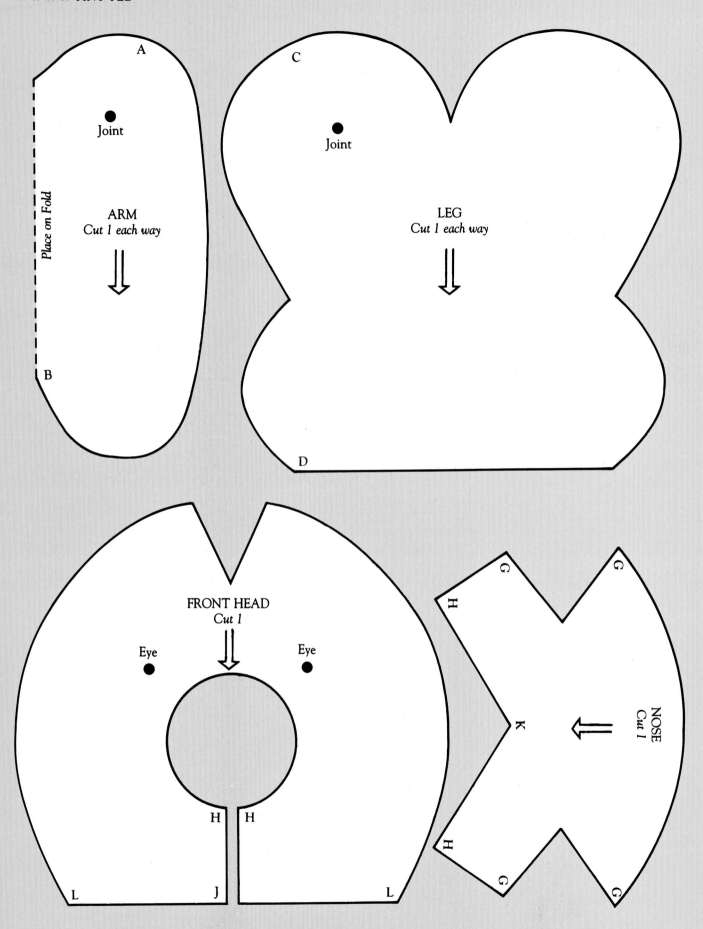

ARM
Cut 1 each way

Place on Fold

Joint

A

B

LEG
Cut 1 each way

Joint

C

D

FRONT HEAD
Cut 1

Eye

Eye

H   H

L   J   L

NOSE
Cut 1

G   G

H

K

H

G   G

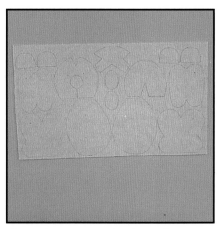

1 Make a pattern of each template shape (see p.5) and draw around it on the wrong side of the fabric, as shown.

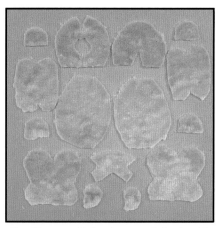

2 Cut out all the pieces and check with the picture that all the sections are there.

3 Items required: 4 joints, 4 large washers, 4 metal safety washers, 2 teddy eyes with washers, and 1 heart nose and washer.

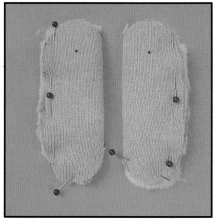

4 With right sides facing, fold the arms in half and pin from **A** to **B**.

5 Stitch along the seam lines of each arm, as shown.

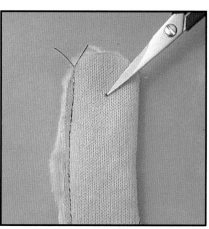

6 Cut a small hole in each arm in the position marked for the joint. Sew round hole.

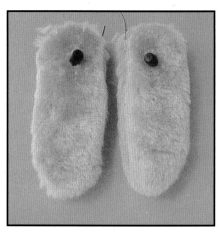

7 Turn the arms right side out and insert a small amount of filling. Insert joint through the hole in each arm (see page 9).

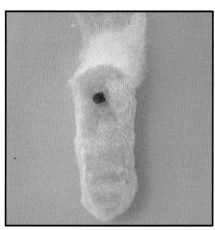

8 Stuff each arm firmly with the filling.

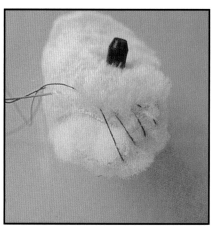

9 Using ladder stitch (see page 8), sew up the openings on each arm by hand.

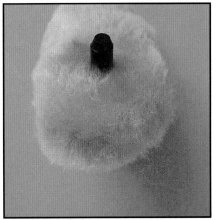

10 Brush the seams on each arm. The picture shows completed arm with joint.

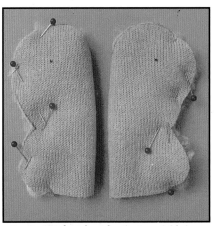

11 With right sides facing, fold the legs in half and pin from **C** to **D**.

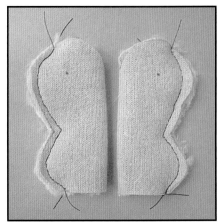

12 Stitch along the seam line on each leg, as shown.

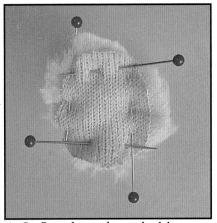

13 Pin a foot pad to each of the openings at the leg ends.

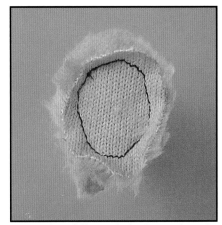

14 Carefully stitch the foot pads to the leg ends around the seam lines, making the circles as even as possible.

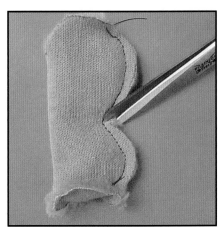

15 Snip the leg seams at the ease points and cut a small hole in each leg in the position marked for the joint. Sew round hole (see page 9).

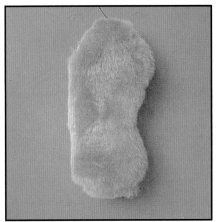

16 Turn both legs right side out.

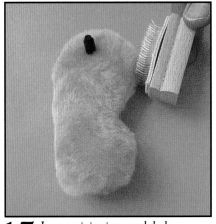

17 Insert a joint into each hole. Continue as for the arms (see steps **8-9**). Brush the seams.

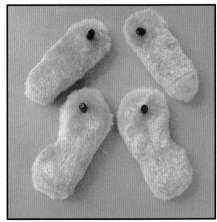

18 Picture shows the 2 completed pairs of arms and legs, with the joints in place.

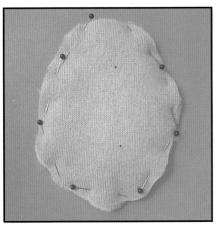

19 *With right sides facing, pin the body pieces together from **E** to **F**, leaving the neck open.*

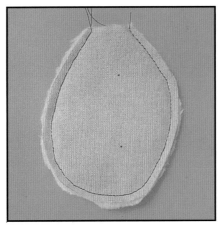

20 *Stitch around the body along the seam line. Cut small holes in the positions marked for the joints. Sew around holes.*

21 *Turn the body right side out and brush the seams.*

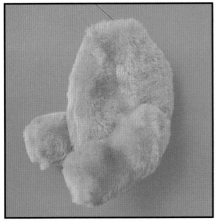

22 *Insert the leg joints into the holes at the lower part of the body and fix (see page 9).*

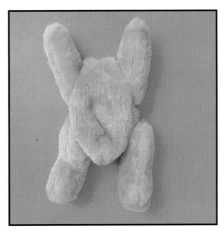

23 *Repeat step 22 for the arms, inserting the joints into the holes in the upper part of the body.*

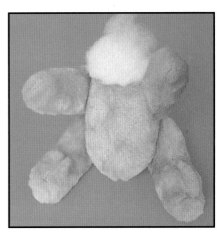

24 *Stuff the body firmly with the filling.*

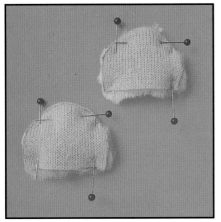

25 *With right sides facing, pin the ear pieces together, as shown.*

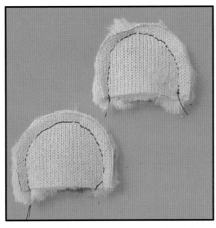

26 *Stitch the ear pieces together along the seam lines, leaving the straight edges open.*

27 *Turn the ears right side out and brush the seams.*

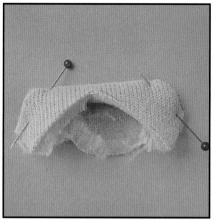

28 *With right sides facing, fold the nose in half and pin the darts from* **G** *to* **G**.

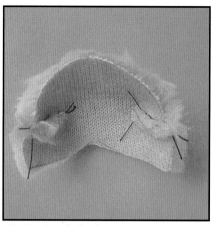

29 *Stitch the darts in the nose from* **G**, *tapering off to nothing, as shown.*

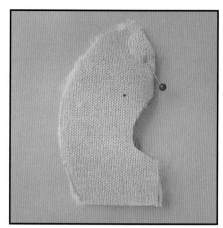

30 *With right sides facing, fold the front head in half and pin the dart.*

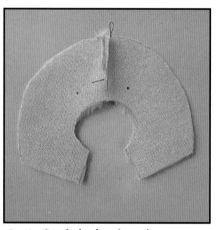

31 *Stitch the dart from the outer edge, tapering off to nothing, and open out the front head piece.*

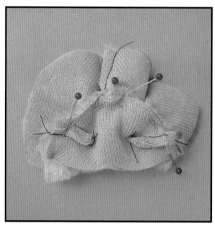

32 *With right sides facing, pin the nose to the front of the head from* **H** *to* **H**.

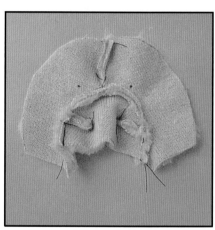

33 *Carefully stitch the nose to the front head along the seam line.*

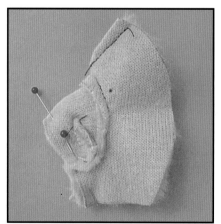

34 *With right sides facing, fold the front head in half and pin from* **J** *to* **K**.

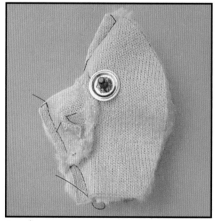

35 *Stitch the nose and front head along the seam line. Insert the eyes (see p.8).*

36 *Insert the nose at position K (see page 8). Brush all the head and nose seams.*

37 To complete the face, embroider a teddy mouth under the nose (see p.8).

38 With right sides facing, fold the back head in half and pin the dart.

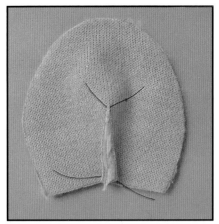

39 Stitch the dart in the back head, starting at the outer edge and tapering off to nothing.

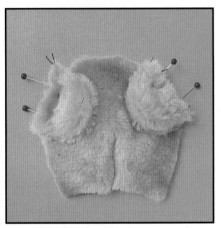

40 With right sides facing, pin the ears to either side of the back head, in the positions marked on the template.

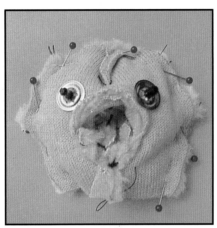

41 With right sides facing, pin the front head to the back head from **L** to **L**, leaving the neck open.

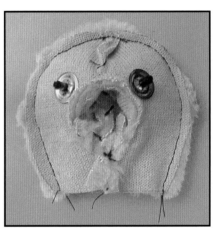

42 Stitch the front head to the back head along the seam line, as shown.

43 Turn the head right side out. Check that the ears are secured in the stitching line.

44 Stuff the head firmly with the filling.

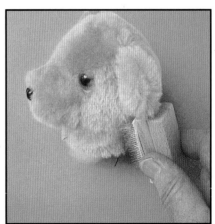

45 Brush all seams in the head.

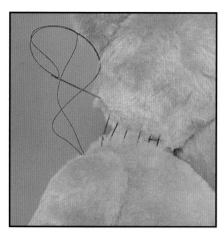

46 Attach the head to the bear's body with ladder stitch (see page 8) and secure.

47 Complete the bear by tying a ribbon around its neck, securing it with a double knot.

48 Tie the ribbon into a bow and cut to the length required.

TREVOR *the* TRADITIONAL TEDDY BEAR ☆☆☆☆☆

MATERIALS

○ Mohair 610mm × 455mm (24″ × 18″)
○ 2 Small Teddy Eyes
○ Black Stranded Embroidery Silk
○ Joints, 5 sets of 35mm (1½″) diameter
○ Ribbon

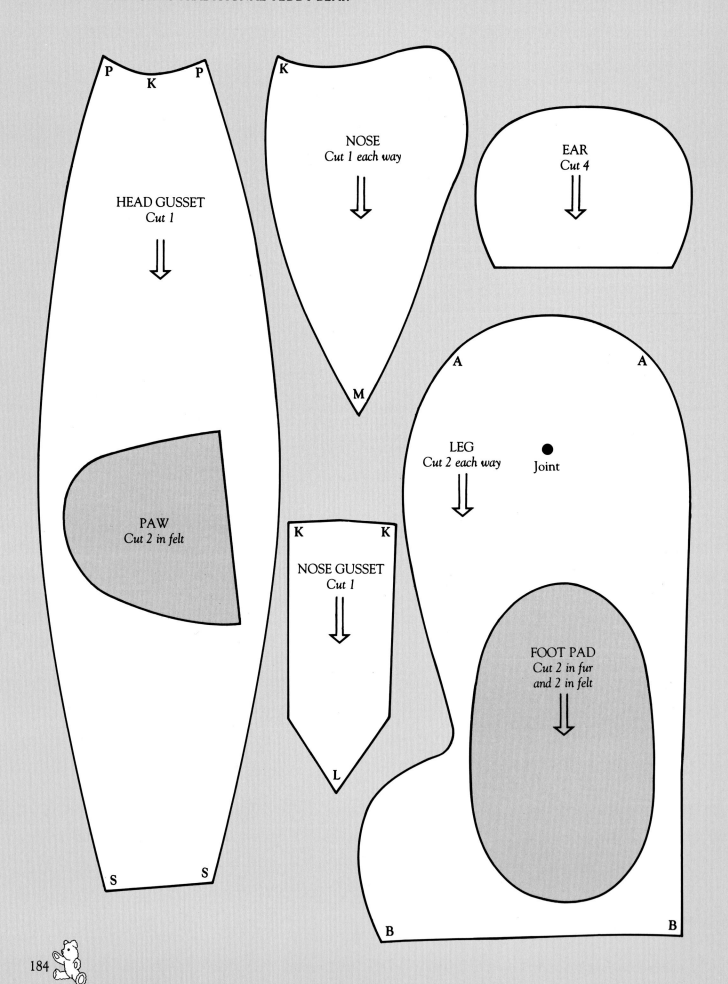

HEAD GUSSET
Cut 1

NOSE
Cut 1 each way

EAR
Cut 4

PAW
Cut 2 in felt

LEG
Cut 2 each way

Joint

NOSE GUSSET
Cut 1

FOOT PAD
*Cut 2 in fur
and 2 in felt*

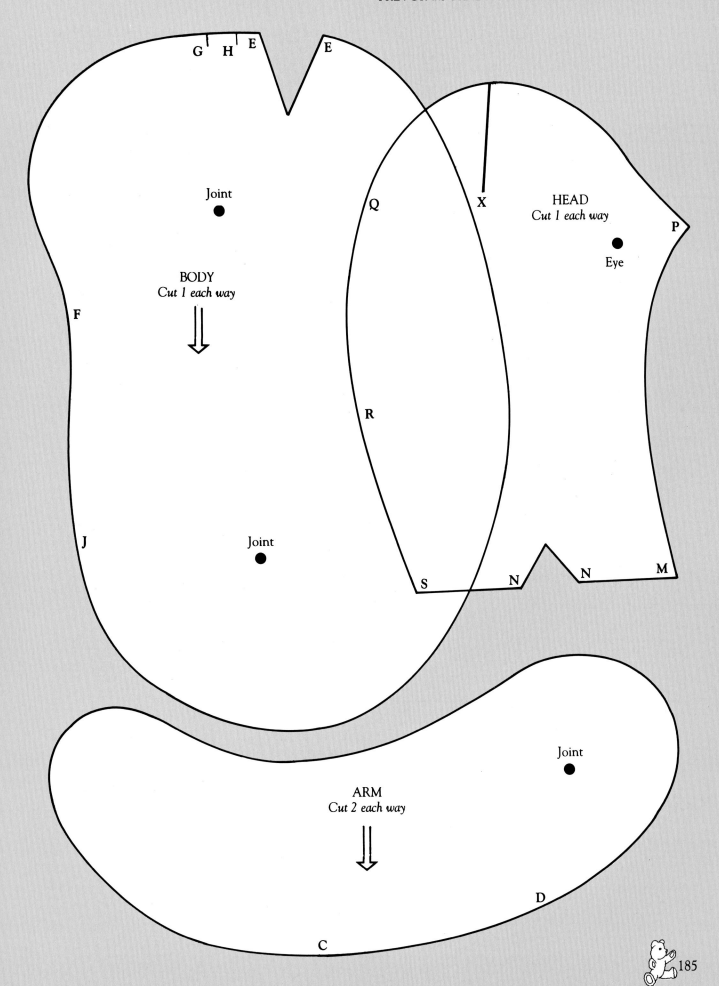

1 Make a pattern (see p.5) and draw around it on the wrong side of the fabric, as shown.

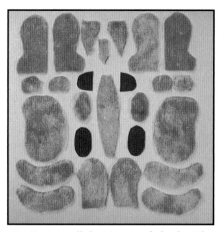

2 Cut out all the pieces and check with the picture that all the sections are there.

3 Items required: skein of embroidery silk, 5 joints, 5 large washers, 5 metal safety washers and 2 teddy eyes with washers.

4 Pin a felt foot pad to the right side of each fur foot pad and tack into place.

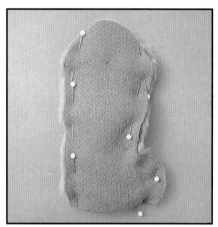

5 With right sides facing, pin 2 leg pieces together from **A** to **B** down both sides.

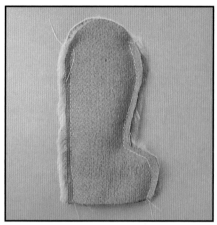

6 Stitch the leg pieces together from **A** to **B** down both sides of the leg.

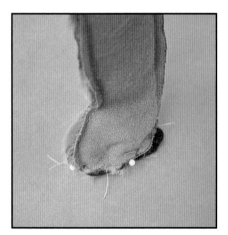

7 With the felt facing the right side of the leg, pin the foot pad to the end of the leg.

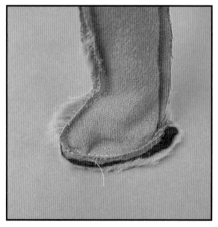

8 Carefully stitch the foot pad to the end of the leg.

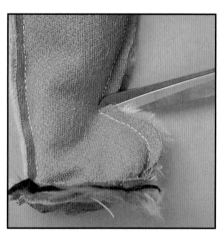

9 Snip the leg seam at the ease point. Repeat steps *4-9* for the other leg.

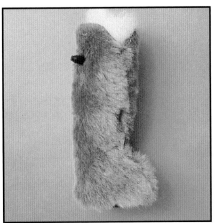

10 Cut a small hole in each leg in the position marked for the joint (see page 9). Insert the joints in the right and left legs. Stuff legs firmly with filling.

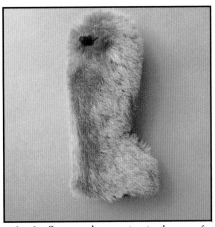

11 Sew up the opening in the top of each leg, using ladder stitch (see page 8). Brush the seams well.

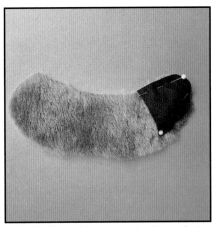

12 Pin a felt paw to the thin end of one arm piece, as shown.

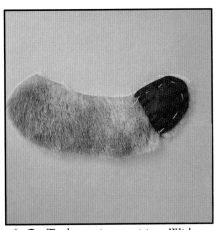

13 Tack paw into position. With matching thread, hand stitch along the straight edge of felt paw. Repeat steps *12-13* to make one right and one left arm.

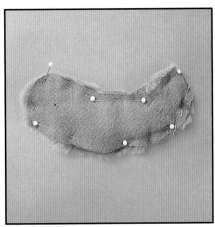

14 With right sides facing, pin the 2 arm pieces to their corresponding outer sides.

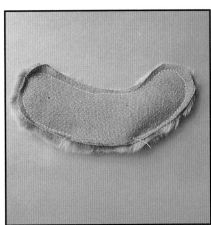

15 Stitch the arm pieces together from **C** to **D**, leaving an opening for turning.

16 Turn the arms right side out and brush the seams. Insert joints in the right and left arms (see page 9) and stuff the arms firmly with the filling.

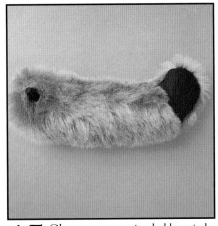

17 Close up arms using ladder stitch (see page 8). Brush the seams well.

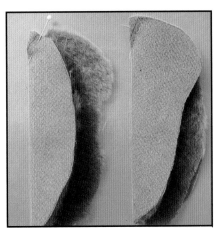

18 With right sides facing, pin and stitch the darts in each body piece from **E**, tapering off to nothing.

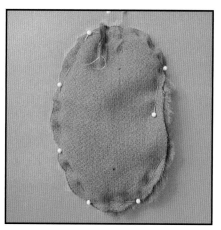

19 With right sides facing, place the body pieces together, matching darts. Pin from **F** to **G** and **H** to **J**.

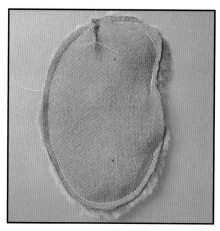

20 Stitch around the body leaving an opening between **F** and **J**, and a small opening between **G** and **H**. Turn right side out and brush seams.

21 Insert limbs in positions marked on the template (see page 9), taking care that each arm and leg is facing the correct way.

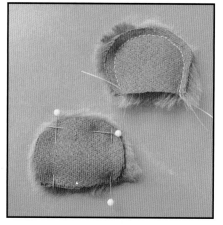

22 With right sides facing, pin and stitch the ear pieces together, leaving the straight edges open.

23 Turn the ears right side out and brush the seams.

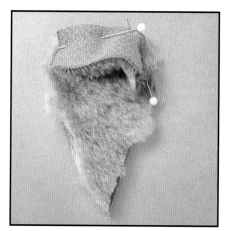

24 With right sides facing, pin the nose gusset to one nose piece from **K** to **K** and continue round to **L**.

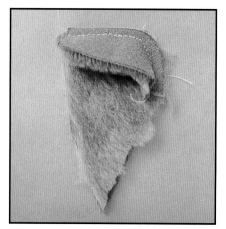

25 Stitch the nose gusset to the nose piece along the seam line, as shown.

26 With right sides facing, pin and stitch the second nose piece to the gusset from **K** to **M**.

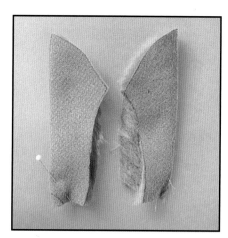

27 With right sides facing, pin and stitch the darts in each head piece from **N** to **N**.

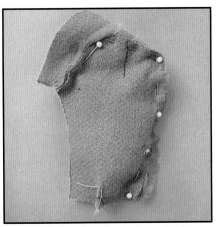

28 With right sides facing, pin the head gusset to the head from **P** to **Q** and **R** to **S**, leaving an opening between **Q** and **R**.

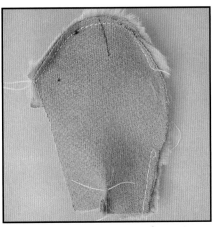

29 Stitch from **P** to **Q** and **R** to **S**. With right sides facing, pin second head piece to gusset and stitch continuously from **P** to **S**.

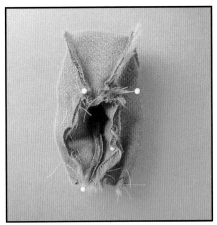

30 With right sides facing, pin the nose to the head from **K** to **M** and from **M** to **K**.

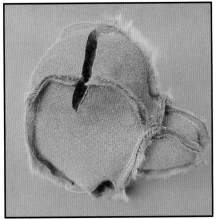

31 Stitch from **M** to **M**. Carefully cut from the bottom of mark **X** on the side head, across the top of the head, to mark on second side, as shown.

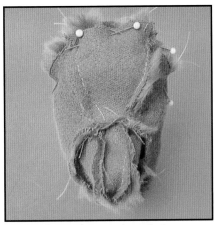

32 Insert the ears through the cut. With right sides facing, pin along the cut, securing the ears between the 2 layers of fabric.

33 Stitch up the opening, tapering off at the ends. Check that the ears are secured in the stitching line.

34 Turn the head right side out and brush the seams. Insert the eyes (see p.8) and embroider the nose and mouth (see p.8).

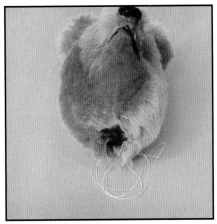

35 Run a gathering stitch around the neck opening.

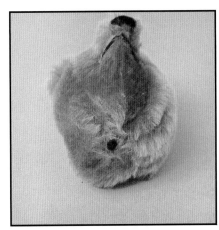

36 Insert a joint into the neck opening, leaving the peg outside. Pull up the thread tightly and secure.

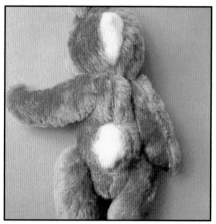

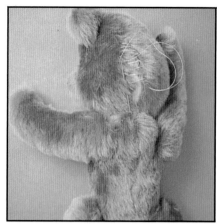

37 *Fix the head to the body by pushing the peg through the small opening in the top of the body. Secure with washers (see page 9).*

38 *Stuff the bear's body and head very firmly with the filling.*

39 *Stitch up the openings in the head and body using ladder stitch (see page 8). Brush the seams well. Complete the bear by tying a bow around its neck.*

Other Mary Ford Titles

Cake & Biscuit Recipes
ISBN: 0 946429 58 8   192 pages
Features over 60 cake and 100 biscuit recipes complete with full introductory pages for the beginner and "Mary's Tips" section to ensure better results.

Children's Birthday Cakes
ISBN: 0 946429 46 4   112 pages
The book to have next to you in the kitchen! Over forty new cake ideas for children's cakes with an introduction on cake making and baking to ensure the cake is both delicious as well as admired.

One Hundred Easy Cake Designs
ISBN: 0 946429 47 2   208 pages
Mary Ford has originated 100 cakes all of which have been selected for ease and speed of making. The ideal book for the busy parent or friend looking for inspiration for a special occasion cake.

A to Z of Cake Decorating
ISBN: 0 946429 52 9   208 pages
New dictionary style home cake decorating book with step-by-step examples covering the techniques and skills of the craft. Suitable for the beginner and enthusiast alike.

The New Book of Cake Decorating
ISBN: 0 946429 59 6   224 pages
The most comprehensive title in the Mary Ford list. It includes over 100 new cake designs and full descriptions of all the latest techniques.

Quick and Easy Cakes
ISBN: 0 946429 42 1   208 pages
The book for the busy mum. 99 new ideas for party and special occasion cakes.

Writing in Icing
ISBN: 0 946429 57 X   96 pages
Full step-by-step guide to over 50 writing styles showing both numbers and letters. The complete guide for the cake decorator to writing on cakes with icing.

Decorative Sugar Flowers for Cakes
ISBN: 0 946429 51 0   120 pages
33 of the highest quality handcrafted sugar flowers with cutter shapes, background information and appropriate uses.

Cake Recipes
ISBN: 0 946429 43 X   96 pages
Contains 60 of Mary's favourite cake recipes ranging from fruit cake to cinnamon crumble cake.

Biscuit Recipes
ISBN: 0 946429 50 2   96 pages
Nearly 100 biscuit and traybake recipes chosen for their variety and ease of making. Full introduction for beginners.

Home Baking with Chocolate
ISBN: 0 946429 54 5   96 pages
Over 60 tried and tested recipes for cakes, gateaux, biscuits, confectionery and desserts. The ideal book for busy mothers.

Novelty Cakes
ISBN: 0 946429 56 1   120 pages
Over 40 creative ideas to make a successful party. Introduction and basic recipes for beginners with full step-by-step guide to each cake design.

Making Cakes for Money
ISBN: 0 946429 44 8   120 pages
The complete guide to making and costing cakes for sale at stalls or to friends. Invaluable advice on costing ingredients and time accurately.

Kids' Cakes
ISBN: 0 946429 53 7   96 pages
33 exciting new Mary Ford designs and templates for children's cakes in a wide range of of mediums.

Jams, Chutneys and Pickles
ISBN: 0 946429 48 0   96 pages
Over 70 of Mary Ford's favourite recipes for delicious jams, jellies, pickles and chutneys with hints and tips for perfect results.

Wedding Cakes
ISBN: 0 946429 39 1   96 pages
For most cake decorators, the wedding cake is the most complicated item they will produce. This book gives a full step-by-step description of the techniques required and includes over 20 new cake designs.

BOOKS BY MAIL ORDER

Mary Ford operates a mail order service for all her step-by-step titles. If you write to Mary at the address below she will provide you with a price list and details. In addition, all names on the list receive information on new books and special offers. Mary is delighted, if required, to write a personal message in any book purchased by mail order.

Write to: Mary Ford,
           30 Duncliff Road,
           Southbourne, Bournemouth,
           Dorset. BH6 4LJ. U.K.